CRIME SCENE INVESTIGATIONS

REAL-LIFE SCIENCE ACTIVITIES FOR THE ELEMENTARY GRADES

PAM WALKER ◆ ELAINE WOOD

Illustrations by Rex Schneider
The Blue Mouse Studio, Gobles, MI

JOSSEY-BASS
A Wiley Imprint
www.josseybass.com

Published by Jossey-Bass
A Wiley Imprint
989 Market Street, San Francisco, CA 94103-1741   www.josseybass.com

Jossey-Bass books and products are available through most bookstores. To contact Jossey-Bass directly call our Customer Care Department within the U.S. at 800-956-7739, outside the U.S. at 317-572-3986 or fax 317-572-4002.

Jossey-Bass also publishes its books in a variety of electronic formats. Some content that appears in print may not be available in electronic books.

Library of Congress Cataloging-in-Publication Data

Walker, Pam.
    Crime scene investigations : real-life science activities for the
elementary grades / Pam Walker and Elaine Wood : illustrations by Rex
Schneider.
        p.   cm.
    ISBN 0-13-084250-8
    ISBN 0-7879-6687-8 (layflat)
    1. Science—Study and teaching (Elementary)—Activity programs.
2. Critical thinking—Study and teaching (Elementary)   I. Wood
Elaine, 1950–   .   II. Title.
    II. Title.
LB1585.W243   1999
507.1—dc21   99-20791

FIRST EDITION
HB Printing 10 9 8 7 6 5

Dedication

This book is dedicated to our families. Our parents, Peggy Walker and J.P. and Helen Rowe, have always encouraged us and supported our efforts. To assist us, they have researched and collected information from every imaginable source. They help us stay abreast of current developments in science.

Matthew, Audrey, and Spencer McGhee are three loving and supportive individuals who have endured us through many projects. Without their constant emotional and physical help, we would have run low on the psychic energy needed to teach school and write at the same time.

Acknowledgments

This book has been influenced by many people. A summer visit to the Georgia Bureau of Investigation was arranged by Margaret Arnold, Douglas County School System's Apprenticeship Coordinator. Scientists, computer experts, fingerprint analysts, and management at the GBI took time out of their hectic schedules to show us everything we wanted to see.

By inviting us to attend our first Biennial Chemistry Conference, Maureen Schuberg provided us with opportunities to learn new science techniques and teaching methods. Through the conference, we met teachers working at all levels of science education who shared their ideas and concerns about increasing student interest in science.

Connie Kallback, our editor, was willing to give us a chance to try something new. She never got tired of answering questions and helping us meet deadlines. Her encouragement and approval kept our spirits high and our pen aimed in the right direction.

Diane Turso, our Development Editor, did an excellent job preparing the manuscript for print. Without her expertise we would not have looked so professional.

Mariann Hutlak, our Production Editor, worked tirelessly to turn the manuscript into a quality publication.

The artwork was beautifully done by Rex Schneider. Rex was able to create Investi Gator and draw the character in interesting investigative poses. Without Rex's creative flair, this book would have lacked some of its appeal.

About the Authors

Pam Walker (B.S., biology, Georgia College; M.Ed. and Ed.S., Georgia Southern University) has 18 years' experience in teaching science in grades 9–12.

Elaine Wood (A.B., biology and secondary education; M.S. and Ed.S., West Georgia College) has conducted research on the cellular and molecular level and has 13 years' teaching experience in secondary science.

Ms. Walker and Ms. Wood teach science at Alexander High School in Douglasville, Georgia. They are co-authors of several teacher resource books, including *Handbooks for Applied Biology/Chemistry* to accompany the CORD modules, *Take Home Experiments* by Frank Schaeffer Publishing, *Scientific Investigations, Science Up to Standards,* and *50 Terrific Science Experiments, Science Super Sleuths,* and *Science Field Trips* by Instructional Fair/TS Dennison. They have also helped fashion a new curriculum for applied science classes by creating two new texts: *Biology in Our Lives* and *Chemistry in Our Lives* from Interstate Publishing. Their earlier science resources with The Center are *Hands-on General Science Activities With Real-Life Applications* (1994), and *Crime Scene Investigations: Real-Life Science Labs for Grades 6–12* (1998).

About This Book

A delightful cartoon character, Investi Gator helps students learn about scientific techniques used by crime scene investigators. Students will learn that investigators are called to the scene of a crime to collect as much evidence as possible. This evidence can include samples of fingerprints, fibers, casts of shoe prints, measurements of crime scenes, and more. Oftentimes, these same investigators help detectives interpret the evidence they have collected. By stepping into the roles of crime scene investigators, students can learn many intriguing scientific strategies and skills.

Crime Scene Investigations: Real-Life Science Activities for the Elementary Grades can be used to supplement and energize your current science curriculum. It is divided into four sections, each one covering a different branch of science: Section 1, "Inquiry, Science, and Technology," reinforces skills of observation, experimentation, and logical thinking. Section 2, "Earth Science," shows how knowledge of the composition of soil and water can influence the outcome of a criminal investigation. Section 3, "Life Science," emphasizes the value of evidence left at crime scenes by living things, focusing on characteristics of hair and skin, skeletal structure, and DNA analysis. Section 4, "Physical Science," uses techniques such as analysis of unknown mixtures and substances to solve a crime.

Each section presents seven or eight separate investigations, which contain the following two parts:

- Teacher Information, including NSTA objectives that apply to the investigation, objectives, approximate time required, materials needed, and answers to the investigation questions

- An investigation, ready for photocopying for each student in the class or group, which includes a brief recounting of the crime, procedure with numbered steps for students to follow, conclusion questions, and other items as required by the investigation, such as data tables or copies of evidence

As students become intrigued and excited by these activities, they learn to take science techniques seriously, allowing them to think like crime scene investigators to solve a mystery. We hope your students will enjoy the challenge of becoming crime scene sleuths.

Pam Walker
Elaine Wood

Contents

◆
_____

SECTION 2
EARTH SCIENCE   67

SECTION 3
LIFE SCIENCE   121

INVESTIGATION 3–3: "Leafing" the Crime Scene
(Comparing Characteristics of Leaves)

INVESTIGATION 3–4: A Spooky Crook
(Assembling a Human Skeleton)

INVESTIGATION 3–5: Pharaoh's Femur
(Using a Bone to Determine a Person's Height)

INVESTIGATION 3–6: One Bite Too Many
(Comparing Teeth Marks)

INVESTIGATION 3–7: Leery of Labels
(Determining Fat Content of Margarine)

SECTION 4
PHYSICAL SCIENCE   191

INQUIRY, SCIENCE, AND TECHNOLOGY

INVESTIGATION 1–1
GRADE TAMPERING

TEACHER INFORMATION

Fingerprints can be fascinating! This investigation requires students to collect and compare the unique characteristics of fingerprints to discover who tampered with a teacher's grade book.

Investigation Objectives:

Collect fingerprints from classmates. Compare fingerprints from crime scene with those of classmates.

Time Required: 50 minutes

Notes for the Teacher:

1. Photocopy Figure 1 found in the Background or sketch it on the board. Discuss the three types of prints with your students. Read the Background to the students, then have them read The Crime.

2. Arrange students in lab groups of four. Give each lab group a copy of the Student Investigator Page.

3. A day or two before class, prepare six or seven strips of lightweight plastic (such as that used in overhead transparencies) that contain fingerprints of one of the students in this class. You might do this by asking one of the students to come by your desk during the day and help you with a "little project" or some other excuse to get him or her to handle the plastic strips. Be certain that the strips do not have any fingerprints on them before the student handles them.

4. In Conclusion Question #6, you might want to specify how much you expect students to write: one paragraph, two paragraphs, or whatever you choose.

Background:

Skin is made of two basic layers: the dermis and the epidermis. The epidermis is on the outside. Penetrating both the dermis and epidermis are hair follicles that contain oil glands. Oil serves an important function in keeping hair and skin soft. The outermost layer of skin is made up of a series of ridges. The skin ridges on every person are arranged in a unique way. These ridges can leave an impression in oil or dirt. Fingerprints are impressions left on surfaces in the oil deposited by that person's touch.

Sometimes fingerprints collected at a crime scene can be instrumental in identifying a criminal. Since most fingerprints are invisible, experts can do one of the following to make them visible:

a. Dust them with a powder. White powder is used on dark surfaces, such as gun stocks or dark boxes. Dark powder is used on light-colored objects, like paper or the toilet handle.

b. Spray them with a chemical that causes the fingerprints to glow in the dark.

No matter how the prints are collected at a crime scene, investigators compare them with prints in fingerprint "banks" to see if they can get a match. If they do, they may know who committed the crime.

These are three basic types of fingerprints: loops, ridges, and whorls. Within each of these types, there are many sub-categories.

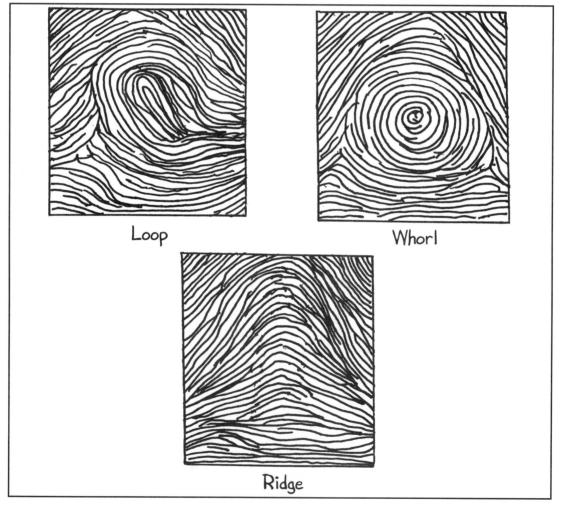

Figure 1. Three basic types of fingerprints are loops, ridges, and whorls.

Materials:

Strips of plastic containing fingerprints
Cornstarch
Small paint brushes
Inkpad
Paper
Tape
Disposable gloves
Small piece (about 4" × 4") of dark-colored construction paper
Magnifying glass (*optional*)
Ruler

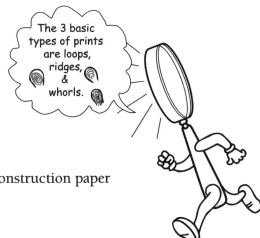

The 3 basic types of prints are loops, ridges, & whorls.

Answers to Conclusion Questions of Investigation 1–1:

1. Answers will vary. If fingerprints of the student who "stole" the grade book page was in a lab group, his or her prints would match someone's prints in the lab group.

2. Fingerprints are impressions of skin ridges left on materials because oil on a person's skin can be transferred to objects that person touches.

3. No.

4. Answers will vary.

5. Answers will vary.

6. Conclusions will vary.

NSTA Objectives that apply to this investigation

As a result of activities in grades K–4, all students should develop:

■ abilities necessary to do scientific inquiry and understanding about scientific inquiry. Students should employ simple equipment and tools to gather data and extend the senses. Students should use data to construct a reasonable explanation. (*Elementary Standard, Science as Inquiry*)

■ abilities of technological design, understanding about science and technology, and abilities to distinguish between natural objects and objects made by humans. Students should understand fundamental concepts and principles that underlie the understanding about science and technology. Tools help scientists make better observations, measurements, and equipment for investigations. They help scientists see, measure, and do things that they could not otherwise see, measure, and do. (*Elementary Standard, Science and Technology*)

As a result of activities in grades 5–8, all students should develop:

■ abilities necessary to do scientific inquiry and understanding about scientific inquiry. Students should use appropriate tools and techniques to gather, analyze, and interpret data. Students should develop descriptions, explanations, predictions, and models using evidence. Students should think critically and logically to make the relationships between evidence and explanations. (Grades *5–8 Standard, Science as Inquiry*)

- abilities necessary to do scientific inquiry and understanding about scientific inquiry. Students should understand fundamental concepts and principles that underlie the understanding about the abilities necessary to do scientific inquiry. Students should use appropriate tools and techniques to gather, analyze, and interpret data. (*Grades 5–8 Science as Inquiry*)

Name _____ Date _____

GRADE TAMPERING
Student Investigator Page

The Crime

Monday morning Mr. Jackson rushes into his classroom frantically searching for his grade book. Over the weekend, he noticed that it was not in his briefcase. Now he's afraid that he might have lost it. As he enters the room, he smiles. There it sits, right on top of his desk. Its protective plastic cover shines under the classroom lights.

Mr. Jackson opens his book and looks through it casually. To his surprise, a page has been torn from the book. Science grades for his second period class are missing. He asks several teachers and students if they saw anyone tampering with his grade book, but no one can help him.

Mr. Jackson decides to collect the prints from the plastic cover on his grade book and compare them with prints of all his students. He hopes to find a match, and therefore find the thief.

Procedure

1. Make a collection of the fingerprints in your lab group.

   a. Decide who in your group will be Student 1, Student 2, Student 3, and Student 4.

   b. Student 1 should gently roll his or her right thumb on the ink pad, then in the Data Table in the appropriate box. Student 1 should repeat this procedure with his or her other nine fingers so that he or she has recorded a complete set of fingerprints in the Data Table.

   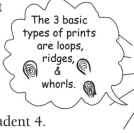

   c. Repeat Step b with Student 2, Student 3, and Student 4.

2. To make the fingerprints on the plastic strip visible, gently paint them with a small amount of cornstarch.

3. Blow away any excess cornstarch, and examine the plastic strip for fingerprints. If necessary, examine it with a magnifying glass.

4. Tear off a piece of tape that is about 3 inches long.

DATA TABLE 1. FINGERPRINTS OF PEOPLE IN THIS LAB GROUP.				
Finger	*Student 1*	*Student 2*	*Student 3*	*Student 4*
Right thumb				
Right index				
Right middle				
Right ring				
Right pinkie				
Left thumb				
Left index				
Left middle				
Left ring				
Left pinkie				

5. Press the sticky side of the tape onto one of the fingerprints.

6. Lift the tape (and fingerprint) from the plastic.

7. Firmly press the tape (and fingerprint) onto a small piece of dark construction paper.

8. Examine the lifted print and compare it with all ten of the prints belonging to Student 1. If you find a match, record the matching finger in Data Table 2.

9. Compare the lifted print with all of the prints belonging to Student 2. Record any matches in Data Table 2.

10. Repeat steps 9 and 10 with fingerprints of Student 3 and Student 4.

DATA TABLE 2. PLACE AN X IN THE BOX TO INDICATE THE FINGERPRINT(S) THAT MATCH ONE OF THE SUSPECT'S FINGERPRINTS.

Finger	*Student 1*	*Student 2*	*Student 3*	*Student 4*
Right thumb				
Right index				
Right middle				
Right ring				
Right pinkie				
Left thumb				
Left index				
Left middle				
Left ring				
Left pinkie				

Conclusion Questions

1. Was the student who tore a page out of Mr. Jackson's grade book in your lab group? How do you know?

_____

_____

_____

2. What is a fingerprint?

   _____

   _____

   _____

   _____

3. Are the fingerprints on all of your fingers the same?

   _____

   _____

   _____

   _____

4. Look at the print of your index finger. Is it a loop, ridge, whorl, or a combination of these?

   _____

   _____

   _____

   _____

5. In the past, only people who were arrested were fingerprinted. Now, many police departments are making fingerprint banks of all citizens in their area. Would you voluntarily give your fingerprints to the police? Why or why not?

   _____

   _____

   _____

   _____

6. Write a conclusion to end the story in The Crime.

   _____

   _____

   _____

   _____

   _____

   _____

INVESTIGATION 1–2

To Code or Not to Code

TEACHER INFORMATION

Students love deciphering the secrets found in coded messages. In this investigation, they learn how to apply the methods of scientific inquiry to write and interpret messages in code.

Investigation Objectives:

Interpret a message written in code.
Write a message in code.

Time Required: 30 minutes

Notes for the Teacher:

1. Read the Background to students, then have them read The Crime. While reading the Background to your students, write some of the code symbols on the board.

2. Copy the Student Investigator Page for each student or for each group of students. This activity is best done in groups of 2 or 3 students.

3. The code used in the note found by Mr. Baker is on the following page. You will notice that the code for the entire alphabet is not discovered in this investigation.

People write in code to keep a message secret. □△○☆Y

Background:

Coded messages have an air of mystery. People usually write a message in code if they want that message to be secret. Two burglars planning a crime might write to one another in code.

A simple way to send a coded message is to write the words backwards. For example, the phrase "key under the flower pot" would be written as "top rewolf eht rednu yek."

11

LETTER	CODE	LETTER	CODE
A	☆	N	⧄
B		O	
C		P	▷
D	⊱	Q	
E	○	R	↓
F		S	
G		T	▭
H		U	▯
I	⊿	V	
J	▷	W	
K		X	
L		Y	
M	▽	Z	

Another way to write a phrase in code is to arrange it so that it must be read in zigzag fashion. That is, start on the left and read the letter on top, then the one below it. Then go to the next letter on top, and continue in that fashion. Can you read the following message?

```
k   y   n   e   t   e   l   w   r   o
  e   u   d   r   h   f   o   e   p   t
```

Most codes are sets of symbols that represent messages. For example, a different symbol can be used to stand for each letter of the alphabet. Numbers are symbols. A simple code that substitutes numbers for letters could be:

```
A    B    C    D    E    F    G    H    I    J   ... etc.
1    2    3    4    5    6    7    8    9   10   ... etc.
```

In this code, the word "hide" is written as "8 9 4 5." To make this type of code a little more complex, three numbers could stand for each letter of the alphabet. For example:

A	B	C	D	E	F	G	H	I	J	. . . etc.
101	102	103	104	105	106	107	108	109	110	. . . etc.

In this code, "hide" is written as "108 109 104 105."

Numbers are not the only symbols that can represent letters. Check out Table 1 for some of the figures that can represent the letter "A." Can you think of others?

TABLE 1. SYMBOLS THAT CAN REPRESENT THE LETTER "A."	
Letter of the Alphabet	**Symbol Used in Code**
A	▯
A	∧
A	⧖
A	⟹

The best known code is the Morse Code. It is made up of a system of dots and dashes that represent letters. The Morse Code was designed to be used on telegraphs, one of our earliest forms of communication over wires. Other codes include the flag signals used by pilots and their landing crew, and the smoke signals once employed by Native Americans.

Materials:

Pencil
Paper

Answers to Procedure Activities of Investigation 1–2:

2. Table 2. Symbols and number of times they occur in message.

SYMBOL	# OF TIMES USED	SYMBOL	# OF TIMES USED
▽	2	◹	1
◯	5	⊱—	1
▭	3	↓	2
☆	1		
◣	2		
▷	2		
▯	1		

3. Code rewritten with "e" substituted for most frequently used symbol.

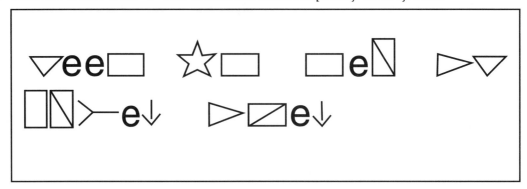

4. Code rewritten with "t" substituted for the second most frequently used symbol.

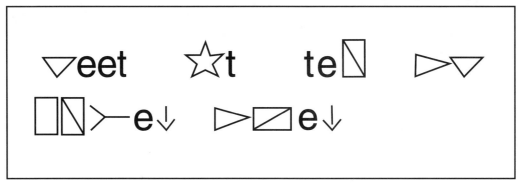

5. Code rewritten with new letters substituted for symbols.

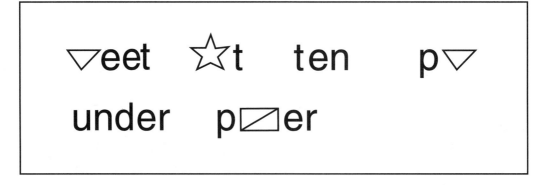

6. Code rewritten with letters you have guessed substituted for symbols.

meet   at   ten   pm

under   pier

7. Table 3. Pieces of the code that are known.

LETTER	CODE	LETTER	CODE
A	☆	N	(symbol)
B		O	
C		P	▷
D	⊱	Q	
E	◯	R	↓
F		S	
G		T	▭
H		U	(symbol)
I	⊿	V	
J		W	
K		X	
L		Y	
M	▽	Z	

8. Answers will vary.

Answers to Conclusion Questions of Investigation 1–2:

1. Answers will vary.
2. Answers will vary.
3. To keep the message secret, or to communicate with someone when conversation is not possible.
4. To communicate, even though they cannot talk.
5. B because pattern of symbols is repeated, like pattern of the message.

NSTA Objectives that apply to this investigation

As a result of activities in grades K–4, all students should develop:

■ abilities necessary to do scientific inquiry and understanding about scientific inquiry. Students should use data to construct a reasonable explanation. (*Elementary Standard, Science as Inquiry*)

■ abilities of technological design, understanding about science and technology, and abilities to distinguish between natural objects and objects made by humans. Students should understand fundamental concepts and principles that underlie the understanding about science and technology. People have always had problems and invented tools and techniques to solve problems. Trying to determine the effects of solutions helps people avoid some new problems. (*Elementary Standard, Science and Technology*)

As a result of activities in grades 5–8, all students should develop:

■ abilities necessary to do scientific inquiry and understanding about scientific inquiry. Students should understand fundamental concepts and principles that underlie the understanding about the abilities necessary to do scientific inquiry. Students should develop descriptions, explanations, predictions, and models using evidence. (*Grades 5–8, Science as Inquiry*)

■ abilities necessary to do scientific inquiry and understanding about scientific inquiry. Students should understand fundamental concepts and principles that underlie the understanding about the abilities necessary to do scientific inquiry. Students should recognize and analyze alternative explanations and predictions. Students should develop the ability to listen to and respect the explanations proposed by other students. (*Grades 5–8, Science as Inquiry*)

Name _____ Date _____

To Code or Not to Code
Student Investigator Page

The Crime

Mr. Baker, President of Space Secret Missions Inc., has found a handwritten note that looks rather strange. He tries to read the note, but cannot. It seems to be written in code. It was found lying in the hall outside his office. Because Mr. Baker and all of his employees take an oath of secrecy, this note is alarming. It might represent an attempt by someone to leak valuable information about the next space mission.

Returning to his office with the note, Mr. Baker examines it again. Mr. Baker knows that the most commonly used letter in the alphabet is "e." So he looks at the message to see if swapping the letter "e" for the most common symbol helps him.

The next most common letter is "t." Mr. Baker places a "t" where he finds the next most common symbol. Eventually, Baker breaks the code and is shocked to read its message. Mr. Baker knows that he must find out who wrote this message. He decides to trick the criminal by sending a message to which only the criminal can respond.

Procedure

1. Examine the coded message below.

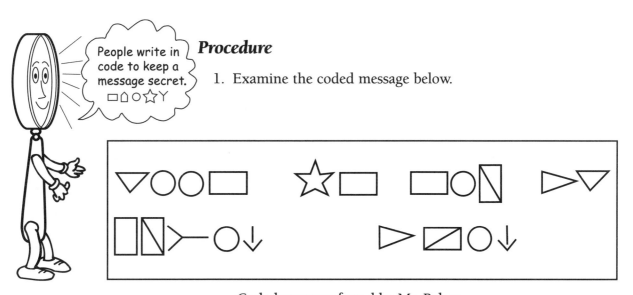

Coded message found by Mr. Baker.

2. Enter each symbol in Table 2. Examine the message and determine how frequently each symbol is used. In Table 2, circle the most frequently used symbol.

TABLE 2. SYMBOLS AND NUMBER OF TIMES THEY OCCUR IN MESSAGE.			
Symbol	**# of times used**	**Symbol**	**# of times used**

3. Rewrite the message, substituting the letter "e" for the most frequently used symbol.

   Code rewritten with "e" substituted for most frequently used symbol.

4. Return to Table 2. Determine the second most frequently used symbol and circle it. Rewrite the message, substituting the letter "t" for this symbol.

   Code rewritten with "t" substituted for the second most frequently used symbol.

5. Late in the evening, Mr. Baker finds a magnifying glass to help him read some very small pencil marks on the note. It seems that someone who knows the code was trying to interpret the message. This is what he sees:

$\square$ = u

$\boxtimes$ = n

$\succ\!\!-$ = d

$\bigcirc$ = e

$\downarrow$ = r

$\triangleright$ = p

Substitute these letters into the coded message.

Code rewritten with new letters substituted for symbols.

6. Based on the parts of the code that you have interpreted, examine the partially decoded message. Are there any words that you can guess? If so, rewrite those words.

Code rewritten with letters you have guessed substituted for symbols.

7. In Table 3, list the codes for the letters that you now know.

TABLE 3. PIECES OF THE CODE THAT ARE KNOWN.			
LETTER	**CODE**	**LETTER**	**CODE**
A		N	
B		O	
C		P	
D		Q	
E		R	
F		S	
G		T	
H		U	
I		V	
J		W	
K		X	
L		Y	
M		Z	

8. You have broken much of this code. Use the code that you know to create a coded message for the author of the note. Your message can be left on the hall floor for that person to find. In your message, suggest a meeting place. The person who appears for the meeting probably wrote the original coded message.

Your message written in code.

Conclusion Questions

1. What was the message of your coded note?

   _____

   _____

   _____

   _____

   _____

2. In this investigation, you used symbols to represent individual letters. Create another code using symbols to represent entire words or phrases. Use this code to write the message "Danger, Danger. Keep out. Enemy nearby."

3. Why might a person write a message in code?

   _____

   _____

   _____

   _____

   _____

4. Why do you think airplane pilots and their ground crew use coded flag signals to direct airplanes?

   _____

   _____

   _____

   _____

   _____

5. Examine the smoke signals below. Which of these interpretations is more likely correct? Why?

   A. "Come to our camp. Meeting of chiefs. Full moon."

   B. "Send help. Buffalo herd near. Send help."

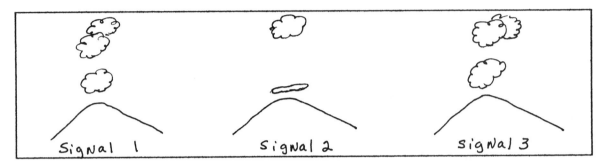

INVESTIGATION 1–3

CORRODED CANS

TEACHER INFORMATION

In this investigation, students work as a team using role cards to determine who is at fault for a corrosive substance found in a soft drink can. They gather data on all the evidence to arrive at an explanation for when or how the corrosive agent was added to the drink.

Investigation Objective:

Working as a team, use data to make a relationship between evidence and explanation.

Time Required: 30 minutes

Notes for the Teacher:

1. Read the Background to students, then have them read The Crime.

2. Arrange students in groups of 8. Copy a set of role cards for each group. Give each student in a group one of the role cards. Tell them that when they read their cards for the first time, they should think about the character they are playing and try to assume some of his or her characteristics. If possible, supply simple costumes or props for students as they assume their roles.

Acids and bases can burn skin.

Background:

Before foods can be placed on the market, they must be approved by scientists at the Food and Drug Administration (FDA). When a foreign substance is found in food, the FDA scientists do experiments to find out the identity of the foreign substance.

Even though it is very rare, corrosive agents have been found in food. Corrosive agents have the ability to break down or destroy some substances. Bases can be corrosive. That means they are basic on the pH scale.

Some mild corrosive agents are found in window cleaner and laundry detergent. A very strong corrosive agent, lye, is found in drain opener. Lye is the common name of a strong chemical, sodium hydroxide. Lye is very dangerous to living things and causes serious burns to the skin.

Materials:

Role cards

Answers to Conclusion Questions of Investigation 1–3:

1. FDA (Food and Drug Administration)

2. A strong base and an ingredient in drain cleaner

3. Causes burns

4. Answers will vary. The corrosive agent could not have been placed in the can at time of manufacture because it burns through cans in about four hours.

5. Answers will vary. Only one can could have held the caustic chemical. The spilled soft drink in the glass container was not caustic enough to have burned the can. Therefore, one can must have held a caustic liquid that was diluted by cola from the other five cans.

6. Answers will vary. That finding would have indicated that all of the cans contained a strong concentration of caustic liquid.

7. Answers will vary.

NSTA Objectives that apply to this investigation

Science and technology have greatly improved food quality and quantity, transportation, health, sanitation, and communication. These benefits of science and technology are not available to all of the people in the world. (*Elementary Standard, Science in Personal and Social Perspectives*)

As a result of activities in grades K–4, all students should develop:

■ abilities necessary to do scientific inquiry and understanding about scientific inquiry. Students should use data to construct a reasonable explanation. (*Elementary Standard, Science as Inquiry*)

As a result of activities in grades 5–8, all students should develop:

■ abilities necessary to do scientific inquiry and understanding about scientific inquiry. Students should be able to think critically and logically to make the relationships between evidence and explanations. (*Grades 5–8 Standard, Science as Inquiry*)

Role Cards

Tom

I was visiting Frank for a few days, and he asked me to go to Bob's party with him. I didn't know Bob or anyone else at his party.

Frank left me in the dining room next to the table of food and drinks. I pulled a can of FizzCo off the six-pack ring and opened it just like I usually do. With the first sip, I felt an instant burning pain. The pain got worse with every passing second. As a matter of fact, it still hurts.

FizzCo should be more careful to keep dangerous chemicals out of their drinks. It was their carelessness that caused my burns. They should pay for my hospital bills and give me extra money to pay for my pain and suffering. I am going to sue them for 1 million dollars!

Frank

Tom is an old friend of mine who lives out of town. He came to visit and I asked him to attend the party at Bob's house.

When we got to the party, I introduced him to some folks, showed him the table of food, and wandered off to talk. Suddenly I heard screaming and turned to see Tom crying out that something was burning him. Man, he was really hurting. Someone called an ambulance, and we got him to the hospital.

I think he'll be OK, but he's mad about the whole thing. I don't blame him.

Sally Siren, Ambulance Paramedic

When we arrived at 9:51 P.M., party guests were trying to help Tom rinse his face and mouth with water. Tom was lying on the floor, screaming.

We put him on a stretcher, and rushed him to the emergency room. A guy at the party told us that Tom was drinking from a FizzCo can when he started yelling.

Once we got on the road, I called the Fire Department and asked them to go to Bob's house and pick up that can. I also called the Police Department so they could find out if foul play was involved.

Fritz Flannigan, Firefighter

A call came in at 10:02 P.M. that there was a "hazardous substance" in a FizzCo can at 502 Simmons Court. We put on our protective clothing and took a small truck to the scene. There was a party in progress. We collected an open can of FizzCo, and five unopened cans. They were all placed in a glass container, the five unopened cans on the bottom and the opened can on top. We took the glass container and cans to the fire station.

We didn't know what to do with the cans, so we left them at the station Saturday night. I noticed on Sunday morning that something had eaten through the bottom of the can stacked on the top and had damaged the other cans. All cans were empty of cola, which had collected in the bottom of the glass container. Someone from the State Crime Lab picked up the whole mess on Monday morning.

Dr. Makewell in the hospital emergency room

I admitted Tom at 10:09 P.M. Saturday night. He was in obvious pain, and large burns were developing on his lips, face, and tongue. I cannot be certain, but they looked like burns caused by a strong acid or base. I gave him something for pain and swelling, and admitted him to the hospital.

He'll be OK, but there may be scarring. Thankfully, Tom didn't actually swallow the cola. That would have damaged his throat, caused it to close, and killed him.

Dr. Allen Analyzer, State Crime Lab

The police called us and said they were sending us some evidence to examine. Monday afternoon, a firefighter brought in a glass container holding six soft drink cans and a lot of brown liquid. The firefighter gave me the history behind these cans. I think that a liquid had eaten through the open can, burned holes in the cans below it, and caused them all to leak their contents.

We analyzed the soft drink in the glass container and found it to be pretty basic; its pH was 10. Soft drinks are usually somewhat acidic, with a pH of 5 or 6.

Dr. Teddy Testtube, FDA Lab

First, I wanted to know how long it would take a very strong acid or base to eat through a soft drink can. Therefore, I put drain cleaner, which contains sodium hydroxide, into an aluminum can in my office and recorded the time. Sodium hydroxide is a very strong base, and it has a pH of 14. In only five hours, the sodium hydroxide had eaten through the bottom of the aluminum can.

The pH of the liquid in the glass container delivered from the fire station was 10. I took some of this liquid and put it in a soft drink can, recorded the time, and set it on my desk. It has been there for four days and nothing has happened to the can yet.

Name _____ Date _____

CORRODED CANS

Student Investigator Page

The Crime

Frank invites his out-of-town friend, Tom, to a party at Bob's house. Tom is only in town for a few days, and Frank does not want to attend the party without him. Tom agrees to go along.

Frank and Tom enter Bob's house, which is swamped with loud and happy people. They make their way to the table where all kinds of food and drinks are arranged. FizzCo soft drinks are stacked in six-packs at one end of the table. Frank introduces Tom to some of his friends, then wanders away to say hello to an old friend. Suddenly, Frank hears a loud scream. When he turns, he sees Tom rubbing his mouth and face, obviously in pain.

An ambulance is called to take Tom to the Emergency Room. Later, the Fire Department picks up the soft drink can from which Tom was drinking and the rest of the cans in that six-pack.

Two weeks after this tragic event, Tom calls the president of FizzCo Soft Drink Company to tell him what happened. Tom explains that his burns are FizzCo's fault, and he plans to sue them. The FizzCo president apologizes, and asks his scientists to investigate this case. The president wants to find out when and how the corrosive agent was added to Tom's soft drink.

Procedure

1. In your group of eight, take one role card. Don't show it to the other students in your group.

2. Read your role card to yourself, and think about the character you are playing. If costumes or props are available, dress your part.

3. Take turns with other students in your group reading your role cards aloud.

4. When everyone has read his or her card, work as a group to determine whether or not Tom's claim is correct: FizzCo was at fault because the corrosive agent was added to the soft drinks during manufacture.

Acids and bases can burn skin.

Conclusion Questions

1. What agency is in charge of testing the safety of food that is for sale?

_____

_____

_____

2. What is sodium hydroxide?

_____

_____

_____

3. How does sodium hydroxide affect the skin?

_____

_____

_____

_____

_____

4. Do you think that the corrosive material was added to the can of soft drink during manufacture or after the can was opened? Explain your answer.

_____

_____

_____

_____

_____

5. How many of the cans in the six-pack do you think held the caustic chemical? Why?

_____

_____

_____

_____

_____

6. If Dr. Allen Analyzer of the State Crime Lab had found the pH of the cola in the firefighter's glass container to be 14, how would that have changed your thinking about the number of cans that contained the chemical? Explain your answer.

_____

_____

_____

_____

_____

7. Based on your findings in the lab, write a paragraph that explains how you think the sodium hydroxide got into the soft drink can.

_____

_____

_____

_____

_____

INVESTIGATION 1–4

BEING HIP TO THE CHIP

TEACHER INFORMATION

Susie is shocked when she parks her new green sports car at the mall and returns to find a large dent in the back. A closer look reveals chips of red paint in the dent. Students run a paint chip analysis on several cars to identify the hit-and-run driver.

Investigation Objective:

Design and conduct an experiment to verify whether or not two paint chips came from the same car.

Time Required: 50 minutes

Notes for the Teacher:

1. Read the Background to students, and have them read The Crime.

2. Copy the Student Investigator Page for each student or for each group of students. This activity is best done in groups of 2 or 3 students.

3. Go to an automobile junk yard. Find 5 red cars, and designate them as car A, car B, car C, car D, and car E. In this case, we'll let car E be the hit-and-run car. Collect 8 chips of paint (each about the size of a dime) from car A, 8 from car B, 8 from car C, and 8 from car D. Collect 16 chips from car E.

   Use the scientific method to solve a problem.

4. Back in the classroom, prepare paint chip samples for each lab group. For each group, label one chip as A, one as B, one as C, one as D, and one as E. Take a second E chip and label it "crime scene."

5. In this investigation, students must develop their own procedure. Place a variety of lab equipment at their disposal, some of which they will need (like microscopes and slides) and some that they will not need.

Before students start working on the investigation, read their proposed procedure. If they suggest doing something that will not answer their question, have them redo the procedure. If their procedure looks good, sign their investigation paper.

Background:

The scientific method is a well-known way of solving a problem or answering a question. The name "scientific" does not imply that only scientists use this technique. People from all walks of life use the scientific method.

To use the scientific method in problem solving, you follow these steps:

1. State a hypothesis. In other words, state the problem or question and guess at its answer. *For example, if you want to know which brand of ice cream, A or B, contains more sugar, your hypothesis could be:*

   Ice cream A contains more sugar than ice cream B.

2. Do some research. Find out what is already known about your problem. *In the ice cream case, read the ingredients label or call the manufacturers to learn more about the amount of sugar in the two brands.*

3. Design and conduct an experiment to test your hypothesis. How will you prove whether your hypothesis is right or wrong? *For the ice cream question, design an experiment to test the amount of sugar in equal quantities of both ice creams.*

4. Gather data. During your experiment, record information that you learn. *In the example, write down your findings from the sugar tests.*

5. Draw conclusions. Study the data you collect and decide if it supports or disproves your original hypothesis. *In our case, look at your experimental results to see if ice cream A contains more sugar than ice cream B.*

6. Report your findings to others. Don't keep your results a secret. Someone else might have the same question. *Call a friend about your ice cream experiment, or report your findings to your class.*

Forensic scientists use the scientific method every day. One type of material that forensic scientists must identify is paint chips. During a hit-and-run accident, a chip of paint can be transferred from one car to another. The crime scene paint chip can be carefully examined under the microscope. If suspect chips are available, they can be compared with the crime scene chip.

A paint chip has three distinctive characteristics:

1. *Color.* There are literally thousands of paint colors.

2. *Layers.* Paint is applied to cars in layers. Some cars may have more than one paint job. Different car manufacturers layer paint in different ways.

3. *Texture.* Two blue cars may not look the same because the texture of the paint is different. Paint texture can vary from shiny and slick to dull and coarse.

Materials:

Crime scene red paint chip from Susie's car
Chip A from John Hewitt's car
Chip B from Elizabeth McGee's car
Chip C from Terry Alexander's car
Chip D from Marlene Gregory's car
Chip E from Deidre Cline's car

Answers to Conclusion Questions of Investigation 1–4:

1. 1. State a hypothesis. In other words, state what you think the answer to the problem might be.

   2. Do some research. Find out what is already known about your problem. If someone else has solved it, you may want to use their information.

   3. Design and conduct an experiment to test your hypothesis. How will you prove whether your hypothesis is right or wrong?

   4. Gather data. During your experiment, record information that you learn.

   5. Draw conclusions. Study the data you collect and decide if it supports or disproves your original hypothesis.

   6. Report your findings to others. Don't keep your results a secret. Someone else might have the same question.

2. 1. One of the most distinctive qualities of a paint chip is its color. There are literally thousands of paint colors.

   2. Paint on cars is applied in layers. Therefore, another quality of a paint chip is its layers.

   3. Texture of paints varies. Therefore, the texture of paint on a paint chip can help identify that chip.

3. Answers may vary. Suspect E was the hit-and-run car.

4. Reports will vary. Students should explain the similarities of the suspect paint chip and the crime scene chip that they identified.

NSTA Objectives that apply to this investigation

As a result of activities in grades K–4, all students should develop:

- abilities necessary to do scientific inquiry and understanding about scientific inquiry. Students should employ simple equipment and tools to gather data and extend the senses. Students should use data to construct a reasonable explanation. (*Elementary Standard, Science as Inquiry*)

- abilities necessary to do scientific inquiry and understanding about scientific inquiry. Students should communicate investigations and explanations. This communication might be spoken or drawn as well as written. (*Elementary Standard, Science as Inquiry*)

As a result of activities in grades 5–8, all students should develop:

- abilities necessary to do scientific inquiry and understandings about scientific inquiry. Students should use appropriate tools and techniques to gather, analyze, and interpret data. Students should think critically and logically to make the relationships between evidence and explanations. (*Grades 5–8 Standard, Science as Inquiry*)

- abilities necessary to do scientific inquiry and understandings about scientific inquiry. Students should understand fundamental concepts and principles that underlie the understanding about the abilities necessary to do scientific inquiry. Students should develop descriptions, explanations, predictions, and models using evidence. (*Grades 5–8, Science as Inquiry*)

- abilities necessary to do scientific inquiry and understandings about scientific inquiry. Students should understand fundamental concepts and principles that underlie the understanding about the abilities necessary to do scientific inquiry. Students should use appropriate tools and techniques to gather, analyze, and interpret data. (*Grades 5–8, Science as Inquiry*)

- abilities necessary to do scientific inquiry and understandings about scientific inquiry. Students should understand fundamental concepts and principles that underlie the understanding about the abilities necessary to do scientific inquiry. Students should design and conduct a scientific investigation. Students should develop general abilities, such as systematic observation, making accurate measurements, and identifying and controlling variables. (*Grades 5–8, Science as Inquiry*)

Name _____ Date _____

BEING HIP TO THE CHIP
Student Investigator Page

The Crime

Susie has taken her new, green sports car to the mall. This is her first outing in the car, and she is excited about driving it. Susie bought the car after saving her money for three years. She spent several weeks picking out the exact color and model that she wanted. Susie parks her car and strolls proudly into the mall.

When Susie returns to the parking lot, she is shocked to see a large dent in the rear of her beautiful green car. A closer look shows chips of red paint in the dent. It's obvious to her that her new car has been hit by a red vehicle.

Susie wanders around the parking lot for about an hour, asking people if they saw the red car or the collision that ruined her car. Finally, she meets Mrs. McConville, who saw the whole thing. Mrs. McConville does not feel confident that she could positively identify the car. However, she is sure that it was an older model Pontiac, and that its paint was dull red.

Mrs. McConville says that after it hit Susie's car, the Pontiac backed up and sped out of the parking lot. Susie calls the police so that she and Mrs. McConville can report the accident. The officers explain to Susie that it may be difficult to find the hit-and-run driver.

During the next week, the police find 5 Pontiacs that fit Mrs. McConville's description:

a. John Hewitt's 1979 Pontiac, which is dented and dirty. John is a student at the local high school, and he drives his car to school and work. He has a job as a sales clerk at the mall.

b. Elizabeth McGee's 1982 Pontiac, whose trunk is filled with packages from the mall where Susie's car was hit.

Use the scientific method to solve a problem.

c. Terry Alexander's 1980 Pontiac, which was recently washed and waxed. Terry drives her car to work every day and claims that she never has time to go to the mall.

d. Marlene Gregory's 1986 Pontiac, which has been in the repair shop all week for body work. Marlene says that last month she ran off the road and hit a tree with her right front fender.

e. Deidre Cline's 1981 Pontiac. Deidre only leaves home once a week, and that's to go to the grocery store. Deidre tells police that she never shops at the mall.

A hypothesis states a problem or a question.

Police officers have taken small pieces of red paint from each car. They submit the 5 suspect paint chips, and the paint chip removed from the dent, to the forensic lab. If they are lucky, the paint chips will help them capture the hit-and-run driver.

In this investigation, you will design an experiment to help find the red car that hit Susie's new automobile. Write your hypothesis in the space below. Then write your experimental procedure and list the materials you will need. If necessary, design some data tables.

Hypothesis

_____

_____

_____

_____

_____

Procedure

1. Develop an experiment that compares paint samples A through E with the Crime Scene paint chip.

2. Write your procedure in the space below, then show it to your teacher. If your procedure is appropriate, the teacher will initial it.

_____

_____

_____

_____

_____

_____

Teacher's Initials _____

3. List the materials you will need for this investigation.

_____

_____

_____

_____

_____

_____

_____

4. On another sheet of paper, create any data tables you need to display the information collected during your experiment.

Conclusion Questions

1. What are the steps of the scientific method?

_____

_____

_____

_____

_____

2. What characteristics of paint chips can be used to identify a particular chip?

_____

_____

_____

_____

_____

3. Were you able to positively identify one of the 5 suspect paint chips as coming from the car that hit Susie's car? _____ Why or why not? _____

_____

_____

_____

_____

_____

Which one did you conclude was the hit-and-run car? _____

4. Complete the following report. It will be used in court to prove that one of the suspect paint chips came from the car that hit Susie's car. In the "Comments" section, explain your findings about color, layers, and texture.

**FORENSIC LABORATORY
REPORT OF PAINT ANALYSIS**

Name(s) of reporting scientist(s) _____

_____

Date _____

Comments on points of comparison between crime scene paint chip and matching suspect paint chip.

    Color _____

    _____

    Layers _____

    _____

    Texture _____

    _____

INVESTIGATION 1–5

TRICKY TOOLS

TEACHER INFORMATION

Someone has stolen Ms. Robin Fowl's binoculars used for class birdwatching. Students in this investigation make a cast of a tool mark left in a door frame and compare it to a suspect's screwdrivers to see if they were used to pry open a locked door.

Investigation Objectives:

Make a cast of a tool mark found at a crime scene. Compare the tool mark cast to the suspect's screwdrivers.

Time Required: Day 1—30 minutes
Day 2—30 minutes

Notes for the Teacher:

1. Before reading the Background to your students, draw a sketch of two different tool marks (shown in Figure 3) on the board. Discuss the differences with your students.

2. Read the Background to students, then have them read The Crime.

3. Arrange students in lab groups of 4.

4. Collect 15 different screwdrivers and label them A, B, C, D, E, F, G, H, I, J, K, L, M, N, O. Let screwdriver F be the one used to commit the crime. In a small piece of clay, make a tool mark of this screwdriver for each lab group. Be sure to make an impression of both sides of the screwdriver.

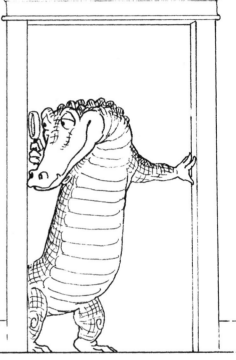

Impressions or cuts caused by tools coming in contact with other objects are called "tool marks."

Background:

Impressions or cuts caused by tools coming in contact with other objects are called "tool marks." Tool marks are generally left by metal tools. For example, a tool mark can be impressed into a wooden door frame as a criminal tries to pry open a locked door (see Figure 2). Tool marks are often found at burglary crime scenes.

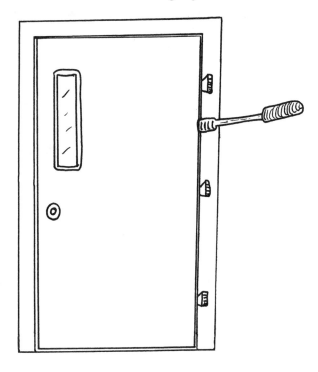

Figure 2. A tool mark can be made in a door frame.

Investigators examine the size and shape of an impression to determine the tool used to make it. (See Figure 3.) When possible, they take the entire object bearing the impression to the lab. However, if the object is too large to move, they make an impression of the tool mark.

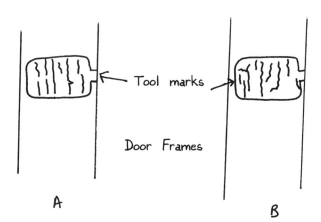

Figure 3. Comparison of tool marks made with two different screwdrivers. Imperfections in the tool make it possible to tell one tool from another.

Tools made of metal often bear unique characteristics. These characteristics may make it possible for investigators to determine what company manufactured the tool. They can then examine that company's records to see which retail stores bought that type of tool. Examination of sales receipts at the retail stores can sometimes reveal who bought that tool at a particular store.

Materials:

Clay
Impression in clay of crime scene tool mark
Suspect screwdrivers confiscated from Mr. Justice's home (A, B, C, D, E), Mr. Refuse's
  home (F, G, H, I, J), and Mrs. Sedan's home (K, L, M, N, O)

Answers to Conclusion Questions of Investigation 1–5:

1. Screwdriver F matched the crime scene tool mark. This one belonged to Mr. Refuse.

2. Impressions or cuts caused by tools coming in contact with other objects are called "tool marks."

3. Tool marks can be made in any wooden surface, such as door frames and window frames.

4. Answers will vary.

NSTA Objectives that apply to this investigation

As a result of activities in grades K–4, all students should develop:

- abilities necessary to do scientific inquiry and understanding about scientific inquiry. Students should employ simple equipment and tools to gather data and extend the senses. Students should use data to construct a reasonable explanation. (*Elementary Standard, Science as Inquiry*)

As a result of activities in grades 5–8, all students should develop:

- abilities necessary to do scientific inquiry and understandings about scientific inquiry. Students should understand fundamental concepts and principles that underlie the understanding about the abilities necessary to do scientific inquiry. Students should think critically and logically to make the relationships between evidence and explanations. Students should be able to review data from a simple experiment, summarize the data, and form a logical argument about the cause-and-effect relationships in the experiment. (*Grades 5–8 Standard, Science as Inquiry*)

- abilities necessary to do scientific inquiry and understandings about scientific inquiry. Students should understand fundamental concepts and principles that underlie the understanding about the abilities necessary to do scientific inquiry. Students should develop descriptions, explanations, predictions, and models using evidence. (*Grades 5–8, Science as Inquiry*)

Name _____   Date _____

TRICKY TOOLS
Student Investigator Page

The Crime

In the spring, Ms. Robin Fowl teaches her students the science of birdwatching. She personally owns a large collection of high-powered, expensive binoculars. Ms. Fowl lets the class use these binoculars on the days they go outside to watch birds.

To make sure her binoculars are safe at school, Ms. Fowl stores them in a cabinet that has a padlock. However, last night someone broke into the school building and stole Ms. Fowl's binoculars. Luckily, clear tool marks could be seen in the wooden cabinet. The tool marks appear to be those of some type of screwdriver.

The classroom doors and windows were not damaged, so investigators concluded that whoever stole the binoculars must have a key to the classroom. People who have a key to Ms. Fowl's classroom include the following:

a. Ms. Robin Fowl

b. Mr. Billy Justice, the principal

c. Mr. Johnny Refuse, the custodian

d. Mrs. Sally Sedan, the auto mechanics teacher

Screwdrivers were confiscated from the homes, cars, and offices of all four people.

Impressions or cuts caused by tools coming in contact with other objects are called "tool marks."

Procedure

1. Make a cast in clay of screwdrivers A–O by firmly pushing each screwdriver into the clay to a depth of about one-half inch. Be sure to make a cast of both sides.

2. Sketch the screwdriver casts in Data Table 1. Be sure to include any nicks or imperfections in the screwdrivers that are revealed in the casts.

3. Sketch the crime scene casts in Data Table 2.

DATA TABLE 1. SKETCHES OF SUSPECT SCREWDRIVER CASTS.		
Mr. Justice's Screwdrivers	*Mr. Refuse's Screwdrivers*	*Mrs. Sedan's Screwdrivers*
A	F	K
B	G	L
C	H	M
D	I	N
E	J	O

DATA TABLE 2. SKETCH OF CAST MADE OF CRIME SCENE TOOL MARK.

Conclusion Questions

1. Who committed the crime? _____

   How do you know? _____

   _____

   _____

2. What is a tool mark? _____

   _____

   _____

3. Name some places a tool mark can be made.

   _____

   _____

   _____

   _____

4. Write a conclusion to the crime story you just solved.

   _____

   _____

   _____

   _____

   _____

INVESTIGATION 1–6

HANDWRITING HOAX

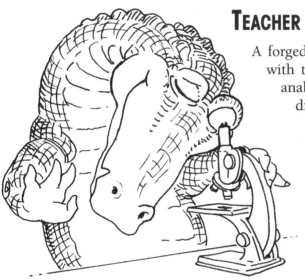

TEACHER INFORMATION

A forged note to a teacher gets students started with this investigation. They use handwriting analysis to figure out which of ten suspects—drawn from some of their classmates—help Susy forge a note to get her out of gym class for the year.

Lab Objective:

Use handwriting analysis to determine who wrote a note.

Time Required: 50 minutes

Notes for the Teacher:

1. Read the Background to students, then have them read The Crime.

2. Copy the Student Investigator Page and Figure 4 from the Background for each student or for each group of students. This activity is best done in groups of 2 or 3 students.

3. A few days before the investigation, ask 10 fellow teachers to provide you with handwriting samples. On one side of an unlined index card, have each person copy the following statement: "Susy loves to participate in gym class. Last year she was exercising and broke her foot. Her doctor would not allow her to take class anymore that year. Sincerely, Mrs. Brown." Have them write their first name on the back of the card.

> Research shows that no two people write exactly the same.

4. One of these volunteers should also write the following sentence on one side of another index card: "Our doctor told us not to allow Susy to exercise the rest of this year in gym class. She has a medical problem. Sincerely, Mrs. Brown." On the other side of this note, write "crime scene."

46

5. Make enough photocopies of the front and back of these cards for each lab group. The day of the lab, every group should be given a card from each suspect and a card taken from the crime scene.

Background:

People often send important information to one another through handwritten notes. Unfortunately, notes can be forged. You may have known of cases where students forged their parents' signatures on school papers or report cards.

Experts can compare a suspect's handwriting with the handwriting of a document in question. Research shows that no two people write exactly the same. When analyzing handwriting, experts compare key points such as slope of letters, spacing of words and letters, crossing of t's and dotting of i's, and closing of e's and o's. Some examples of points to compare in handwriting analysis are illustrated in Figure 4.

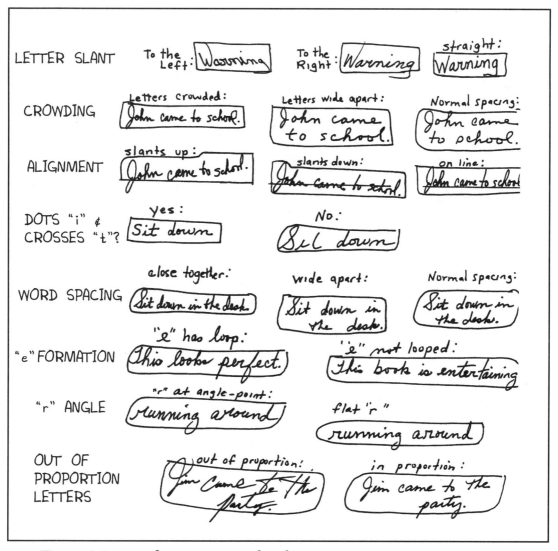

Figure 4. Points of comparison in handwriting.

Materials:

Magnifying glass
Samples of handwriting from each suspect
Handwriting on note to gym teacher (crime scene)

Answers to Conclusion Questions of Investigation 1–6:

1. Yes. One of the suspect's handwriting had several points of similarity to the crime scene note.

2. Answers will vary.

3. Answers will vary.

NSTA Objectives that apply to this investigation

As a result of activities in grades K–4, all students should develop:

■ abilities necessary to do scientific inquiry and understanding about scientific inquiry. Students should use data to construct a reasonable explanation. (*Elementary Standard, Science as Inquiry*)

As a result of activities in grades 5–8, all students should develop:

■ abilities necessary to do scientific inquiry and understandings about scientific inquiry. Students should use appropriate tools and techniques to gather, analyze, and interpret data. Students should think critically and logically to make the relationships between evidence and explanations. (*Grades 5–8 Standard, Science as Inquiry*)

■ abilities necessary to do scientific inquiry and understandings about scientific inquiry. Students should understand fundamental concepts and principles that underlie the understanding about the abilities necessary to do scientific inquiry. Students should think critically and logically to make the relationships between evidence and explanations. Students should be able to review data from a simple experiment, summarize the data, and form a logical argument about the cause-and-effect relationships in the experiment. (*Grades 5–8 Standard, Science as Inquiry*)

■ abilities necessary to do scientific inquiry and understandings about scientific inquiry. Students should understand fundamental concepts and principles that underlie the understanding about the abilities necessary to do scientific inquiry. Students should develop descriptions, explanations, predictions, and models using evidence. (*Grades 5–8, Science as Inquiry*)

Name _____ Date _____

HANDWRITING HOAX
Student Investigator Page

The Crime

Before school, Susy Brown presents a note from her parents to her gym teacher. The note indicates that Susy should not exercise in gym class due to a medical problem. Mrs. Wilkes, the gym teacher, suspects that the note may not have been written by Susy's parents.

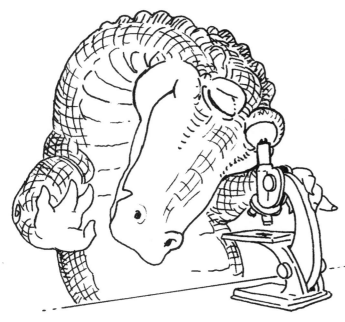

After questioning, Susy admits that an older student wrote the note. But Susy does not want to tell the name of that student. She does, however, indicate the student's grade level. The principal calls in ten of Susy's older friends and asks them for their help. He instructs each of these older students to write a sentence on a card and place his or her first name on the back of the card. The principal then compares these sentences with the note Susy brought to the gym teacher.

Research shows that no two people write exactly the same.

Procedure

1. Obtain a handwriting sample from each suspect and a copy of the note to the gym teacher.

2. Complete Data Table 1 with your analysis of nine samples of handwriting. Use your magnifying glass if you need a closer look. An example is done for you in the second column. Use Figure 4 to help you fill in the chart.

DATA TABLE 1.

	Example	Crime scene note	Suspect 1	Suspect 2	Suspect 3	Suspect 4	Suspect 5	Suspect 6	Suspect 7	Suspect 8	Suspect 9	Suspect 10
slant of letters	*right*											
crowding	*normal*											
alignment	*on line*											
i's and t's	*crosses but does not dot*											
word spacing	*close*											
pressure	*normal*											
e loops	*not looped*											
angle of r	*pointed*											
unique letters	*none unique*											
proportions	*in proportion*											

Conclusion Questions

1. Did one of the suspects commit the crime? Explain your answer.

_____

_____

_____

_____

2. In the following spaces, have each person in the group write the following sentence: "Handwriting can be a clue to finding a criminal." Sign your name after the sentence.

_____

_____

_____

_____

_____

_____

3. Use the information given in the Background to analyze the handwriting samples in question # 2. Record your analysis in Data Table 2.

DATA TABLE 2.	
Name of writer	**Notes experts might make about this person's handwriting**

INVESTIGATION 1–7
PUTTING THE WRONG FOOT FORWARD

TEACHER INFORMATION

To conduct this investigation, students make a cast of a shoe print and compare it to the bottom of a suspect's shoe to discover who sprayed shaving cream on a teacher's car in the parking lot.

Investigation Objectives:

Make a plaster cast of a shoe print. Compare the suspect's shoe to the plaster cast.

Time Required:

Two 50-minute periods

Notes for the Teacher:

1. Read the Background to students, then have them read The Crime.

2. Copy the Student Investigator Page and Figure 5 from the Background for each student or for each group of students. This activity is best done in groups of 2 or 3 students.

3. A week before the activity, ask each student to bring one old tennis shoe to school. Each student bringing a shoe should write his or her name on a piece of paper and tape it inside of the shoe he or she brings. Also collect enough shoe boxes to provide one for each group. You do not need the lids.

4. On the morning of this activity, dampen the ground where the activity will occur. Select one of the shoes brought in by students and make as many shoe prints in the dirt/mud as there are student groups. After making the prints, clean the shoe and place it with the others.

5. Use the box of Plaster of Paris to write mixing directions on the board for your students.

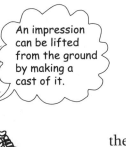

An impression can be lifted from the ground by making a cast of it.

Background:

If the ground is soft or moist, an impression of an object can be left where it touches the earth. An impression is a copy made when an object presses into something soft.

Shoe marks and tire prints are impressions often left at crime scenes. An impression can be lifted from the ground by making a cast of it. A cast is made by pouring a casting material into the impression and allowing it to harden. Plaster of Paris and dental stone are two substances that will harden after being mixed with water. They are often used to make casts.

A cast needs to dry for 24 to 48 hours before being removed from the ground. Before pouring the Plaster of Paris into an impression, the inside of the impression can be sprayed with a light coat of wax. This is done so that the hardened cast will be easy to remove.

When comparing a cast to a piece of evidence that has been collected from a suspect, there are several things to consider. Size, shape, and design are taken into account along with any nicks or gouges in the item examined. If there are enough points of similarity between the cast and the piece of evidence, you may have a match.

Materials:

15 tennis shoes
Empty shoe box with the bottom removed
Plaster of Paris
Water
Unlined white paper
Wooden stick
Disposable plastic cup
Hair spray

Answers to Conclusion Questions of Investigation 1–7:

1. Answer depends on which student's shoe you used to make the cast.

2. Answers will vary. Shoes of obviously different size and shape are easy to rule out.

3. Answers will vary, depending on the shoe you used.

4. No. Impressions are not made in hard materials like dry soil. It's easy to make impressions in soft, damp earth.

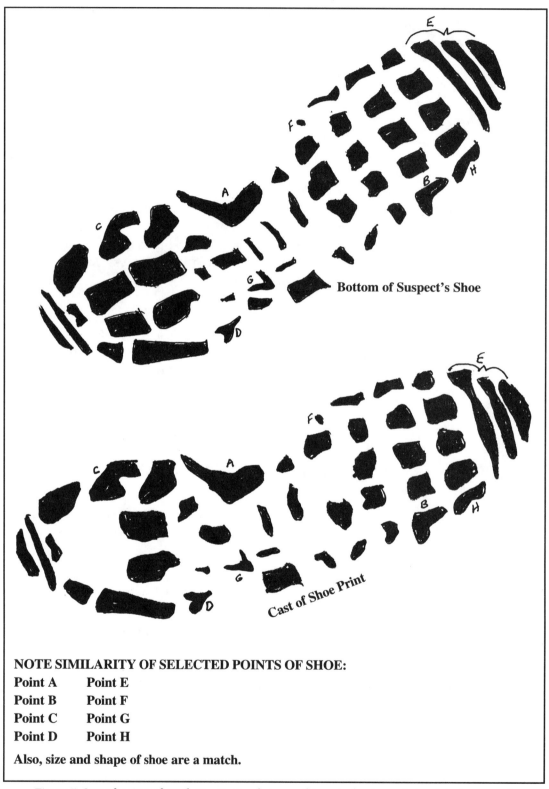

NOTE SIMILARITY OF SELECTED POINTS OF SHOE:

Point A   Point E
Point B   Point F
Point C   Point G
Point D   Point H

Also, size and shape of shoe are a match.

Figure 5. Several points of similarity are seen between this cast of a shoe print and the bottom of a suspect's shoe.

NSTA Objectives that apply to this investigation

As a result of activities in grades K–4, all students should develop:

- abilities necessary to do scientific inquiry and understanding about scientific inquiry. Students should employ simple equipment and tools to gather data and extend the senses. Students should use data to construct a reasonable explanation. (*Elementary Standard, Science as Inquiry*)

- abilities necessary to do scientific inquiry and understanding about scientific inquiry. Students should use data to construct a reasonable explanation. (*Elementary Standard, Science as Inquiry*)

- abilities necessary to do scientific inquiry and understanding about scientific inquiry. Students should communicate investigations and explanations. This communication might be spoken or drawn as well as written. (*Elementary Standard, Science as Inquiry*)

As a result of activities in grades 5–8, all students should develop:

- abilities necessary to do scientific inquiry and understanding about scientific inquiry. Students should understand fundamental concepts and principles that underlie the understanding about the abilities necessary to do scientific inquiry. Students should think critically and logically to make the relationships between evidence and explanations. Students should be able to review data from a simple experiment, summarize the data, and form a logical argument about the cause-and-effect relationships in the experiment. (*Grades 5–8 Standard, Science as Inquiry*)

- abilities necessary to do scientific inquiry and understanding about scientific inquiry. Students should understand fundamental concepts and principles that underlie the understanding about the abilities necessary to do scientific inquiry. Students should develop descriptions, explanations, predictions, and models using evidence. (*Grades 5–8, Science as Inquiry*)

- abilities necessary to do scientific inquiry and understanding about scientific inquiry. Students should understand fundamental concepts and principles that underlie the understanding about the abilities necessary to do scientific inquiry. Students should use appropriate tools and techniques to gather, analyze, and interpret data. (*Grades 5–8, Science as Inquiry*)

- abilities necessary to do scientific inquiry and understanding about scientific inquiry. Students should understand fundamental concepts and principles that underlie the understanding about the abilities necessary to do scientific inquiry. Students should design and conduct a scientific investigation. Students should develop general abilities, such as systematic observation, making accurate measurements, and identifying and controlling variables. (*Grades 5–8, Science as Inquiry*)

Name _____   Date _____

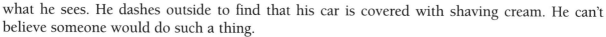

PUTTING THE WRONG FOOT FORWARD
Student Investigator Page

The Crime

Mr. Swanson teaches sixth-grade science at Benton Middle School. He is the proud owner of a new, red sports car. He is so proud of his new car that he parks it right outside the door of his room!

During his afternoon planning period, Mr. Swanson peeks outside to check on his shiny new car and is shocked at what he sees. He dashes outside to find that his car is covered with shaving cream. He can't believe someone would do such a thing.

As Mr. Swanson looks around his car for evidence, he sees many small footprints. Mr. Swanson knows his car was okay at 11:00 because he checked on it then. The only students who have been on his side of the building since 11:00 belong to Mrs. Jones's class. They walk to the lunchroom at 11:20. He suspects that the culprit must be in Mrs. Jones's class right now.

Mr. Swanson telephones the principal and Mrs. Jones and explains the situation to them. They agree to go along with Mr. Swanson's plan to capture the criminal.

Mr. Swanson asks each of the 15 students in Mrs. Jones's class to remove one shoe, put his or her name inside of it, and place it on the floor in the middle of the room. Your job is to help Mr. Swanson determine if one of the shoes fits the print near his car. You will make a cast of the crime scene print and compare it with the shoes in the middle of the room.

An impression can be lifted from the ground by making a cast of it.

Procedure

Day 1, Part A

1. Following your teacher's directions, prepare your mixture of Plaster of Paris in the disposable plastic cup.

2. Go outdoors with your teacher and locate a footprint in the area where the crime was committed.

3. Place the shoe box around the print and press the box into the mud.

4. Spray the print lightly with hair spray.

5. Pour your Plaster of Paris mixture into the print until the mixture completely covers the top of the print and meets all four sides of the shoe box.

6. Go indoors and allow the cast to dry.

Day 1, Part B

Complete Data Table 1 concerning the shoes in the middle of the room. In the Data Table place the name of each shoe's owner, a sketch of the sole of the shoe, the length of the shoe, the width of the shoe (at the widest point), and any comments about the shoe. Do this for all 15 suspects' shoes. In the comment section, note any irregularities on the bottom of the shoe or any special designs.

DATA TABLE 1. INFORMATION ABOUT THE SUSPECT'S SHOES.				
Student name inside shoe	*Sketch of sole of shoe*	*Length of shoe at widest point*	*Width of shoe at widest point*	*Comments about the shoe*
Example: Sue		*10 cm*	*27 cm*	*Nike™ emblem on bottom of shoe— worn down on upper big toe side*

DATA TABLE 1. INFORMATION ABOUT THE SUSPECT'S SHOES. *(cont.)*				
Student name inside shoe	*Sketch of sole of shoe*	*Length of shoe at widest point*	*Width of shoe at widest point*	*Comments about the shoe*

Day 2, Part C

1. Go outside, remove your cast from the ground, and bring it indoors.

2. Measure the length and width of the shoe for which you made the cast. In Data Table 2, sketch the bottom of the shoe cast and make comments about the shoe.

Criminal	Sketch	Length	Width	Comments

DATA TABLE 2. INFORMATION ON CAST OF CRIMINAL'S SHOE.

Conclusion Questions

1. Who was the criminal? Explain your answer.

   _____

   _____

   _____

   _____

2. Which shoes were you able to rule out immediately? Why?

   _____

   _____

   _____

   _____

3. Were there any irregular marks or designs on the bottom of the criminal's shoe that helped you make that determination?

   _____

   _____

   _____

4. Would this investigation have been possible if the ground had not been damp the day of the crime? Explain your answer.

_____

_____

_____

_____

_____

_____

_____

_____

TEACHER INFORMATION

In this investigation, the class must help a student, Sally, who has been gathering data on her computer by taking statements from the theft suspects. When Sally accidentally hits a wrong key and scrambles all the data, the class must help organize the facts in the order in which they occurred.

Investigation Objective:

Organize evidence in proper sequence.

Time Required: 50 minutes

Notes for the Teacher:

1. Read the Background to students, then have them read The Crime.
2. Copy the Student Investigator Page for each student.

Background:

Organizing evidence is an important part of solving crimes. Details about specific times and places are vital in a criminal case. When the case comes to trial, lawyers closely question witnesses about their memory of events.

Since some cases are not brought to trial for several months, witnesses may forget specific details. This is why witnesses are interviewed by police immediately after a crime. Each piece of information the witness provides is recorded for future use.

Details about specific times and places are vital to criminal cases.

Materials:

Scissors
Clear tape
Plain white paper

Answers to Conclusion Questions of Investigation 1–8:

1. Since some criminal cases are not brought to trial for several months, witnesses may forget specific details. Recording this information allows it to be used as evidence in trials.

2. 2 days

3. Yes. You would not be able to tell how many days these events covered.

4. (1) After school on January 14 when Sue and Mary were cleaning the room, and (2) When Mr. Roden opened Mrs. Jackson's classroom 5 minutes before students returned from lunch on January 14.

5. Answers will vary.

NSTA Objectives that apply to this investigation

As a result of activities in grades K–4, all students should develop:

■ abilities necessary to do scientific inquiry and understanding about scientific inquiry. Students should use data to construct a reasonable explanation. (Elementary Standard, Science as Inquiry)

■ abilities necessary to do scientific inquiry and understanding about scientific inquiry. Students should communicate investigations and explanations. This communication might be spoken or drawn as well as written. (Elementary Standard, Science as Inquiry)

As a result of activities in grades 5–8, all students should develop:

■ abilities necessary to do scientific inquiry and understanding about scientific inquiry. Students should understand fundamental concepts and principles that underlie the understanding about the abilities necessary to do scientific inquiry. Students should use appropriate tools and techniques to gather, analyze, and interpret data. (Grades 5–8, Science as Inquiry)

Name _____ Date _____

DISORGANIZED DATA
Student Investigator Page

The Crime

Recently, Mrs. Jackson's gold coin collection was stolen from school. Two suspects, Mary and Sue, were accused of the crime. The gold coins were eventually recovered and returned to Mrs. Jackson, so she did not press criminal charges.

To teach a lesson to all the students, the principal decided that a schoolwide trial should be conducted. A trial date was set and students were given such jobs as defense attorney, prosecuting attorney, judge, and jury. Sally was appointed to take statements from individuals involved in the theft. She prepared these statements on her computer.

On the morning of the trial, Sally made a terrible error. Before she had a chance to save her work on the computer, she accidentally hit the wrong key and scrambled all the facts. Sally has only one hour to straighten out this mess.

Use your powers of logic and reason to help Sally put the facts in order. If you cannot help her, a year of hard work will be lost for everyone. Sue and Mary will be declared innocent due to lack of evidence.

Procedure

1. Use scissors to cut apart each of the 25 clues on the "Disorganized Data Worksheet."

2. Read each clue, then arrange them in a logical order. Remember that sequencing is very important in this case.

3. Once you determine the order, tape the clues in the correct sequence from the top to the bottom of the paper, then number them.

Details about specific times and places are vital to criminal cases.

Disorganized Data Worksheet

* The bell sounds and class is dismissed at 3:02 P.M.

* Mrs. Taft locks the classroom door.

* Mrs. Taft turns off the lights in the classroom.

* Mrs. Jackson clocks in at 7:45 A.M. on January 14.

* Mrs. Taft steps across the hall to Mr. Roden's classroom to see if he has a key that she can use to lock the door.

* On the afternoon of January 15, Mary, Sue, their parents, the principal, and Mrs. Jackson have a conference about the gold coin theft.

* Mrs. Jackson arrives at school and parks her Isuzu Rodeo in space 34 on January 14. The time is about 7:37 A.M.

* Mrs. Taft comes back to Mrs. Jackson's room with the door key and notices that Mary and Sue are gone.

* Mrs. Jackson enters her room, opens the top desk drawer, and sees that her gold coin collection is missing.

* Mrs. Jackson parks her car in space 34 on January 15. The time is about 7:25 A.M.

* Sue and Mary stay after school on January 14 to help Mrs. Taft clean up.

* Sue and Mary are called to the principal's office at 9:00 A.M. on January 15.

* Mrs. Taft clocks out for the day. The time clock reads 3:45 P.M.

* Mrs. Jackson clocks in at 7:45 A.M. on January 14.

* Mrs. Taft clocks in on January 14 at 12:10 P.M.

* Mr. Roden opens Mrs. Jackson's classroom with his key five minutes before students return from lunch.

* Mrs. Jackson begins to feel very nauseated this morning.

* Mr. Zimmer calls Mrs. Taft and asks her if she can come in immediately to sub for Mrs. Jackson.

* Mrs. Taft teaches Mrs. Jackson's last two science classes of the day.

* Mr. Roden is not in his room when Mrs. Taft peeks in his classroom door to look for a key.

* The principal finds Mrs. Jackson's gold coin collection in the gym locker room. It is in a locker that Sue and Mary share.

* Mrs. Taft is thrilled to see the classroom door is already unlocked for her after lunch.

* A little before noon Mrs. Jackson tells the principal, Mr. Zimmer, that she is sick and needs to go home.

* Mrs. Taft walks to the principal's office and gets a key to the room.

* Mrs. Taft reviews Mrs. Jackson's lesson plans.

Conclusion Questions

1. Explain why it is important to have information about a crime organized in logical order.

   _____

   _____

   _____

   _____

2. How many days did the information in this investigation cover?

   _____

   _____

3. Would this have been more difficult if some dates and times had not been given? Explain your answer.

   _____

   _____

   _____

   _____

4. Name two possible times during January 14 when the gold coins could have been stolen.

   _____

   _____

   _____

   _____

5. If you were the jury reading this information after it was organized, would you think Sue and Mary were innocent or guilty? Write a conclusion to this story in which you describe who you think committed the crime and why. If you think it was Sue and Mary, indicate what data helped you decide.

   _____

   _____

   _____

   _____

   _____

   _____

SECTION 2

♦

EARTH SCIENCE

INVESTIGATION 2–1
THE SOIL EVIDENCE

TEACHER INFORMATION

Someone pried open the trunk of Mr. Sullivan's car and stole the football game admission money. Students solve the crime by comparing similarities and differences in soil samples at the crime scene to samples scraped off the suspect's shoes.

Investigation Objectives:

Design an experiment to link soil evidence found on a suspect to a crime scene.

Time Required: 50 minutes

Notes for the Teacher:

1. Read the Background to students, then have them read The Crime. After reading the Background to your students, demonstrate—according to figures 6 and 7—how to test for pH and how to determine the water-holding ability of soil.

2. Arrange students in groups of 2, 3, or 4. Give each group a copy of the Student Investigator Page.

Use the scientific method to solve a problem.

3. This investigation requires that students develop their own procedure and list of materials, and create any data tables they need. Some suggestions for procedures are given in the Background. This investigation should not be attempted by students who haven't done some soil analysis work before. Before students begin the investigation, read the Procedure that they write. If students are proposing to do something that will not answer their questions, have them redo their Procedure. If the Procedure is satisfactory, sign their investigation paper and let them get started.

4. Make a variety of lab equipment available for the class to use in this activity.

5. Prior to the day of the investigation, collect the following different soil samples:

   Sample A—3 cups of soil

   Sample B—3 cups of soil from a different location

   Sample C—3 cups of soil from another location

   Sample CS (crime scene)—another 3 cups of soil from the C location

Background:

Soil evidence can be a valuable tool in linking a suspect to a crime scene. If the soil at a crime scene is unique to the area, it can be identified after it is transferred from the crime. Almost anyone who is present at a crime scene affects the scene by picking up or leaving materials.

There are several ways to find similarities in two soil samples. One way is by comparing the pH of each soil sample. You may remember that pH is a measure of how acidic or basic a material is. Acidity of soil can be determined in several ways. One simple test for soil pH is to add 100 ml of water to a small soil sample, stir, then pour the water and soil through a funnel lined with filter paper. The water collected below the funnel can be checked with pH paper (see Figure 6).

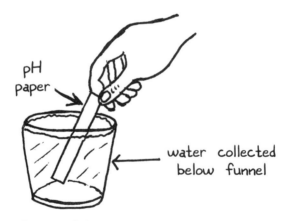

Figure 6. Checking the pH of the water with pH paper.

An investigator can also compare the water-holding capacities of two soil samples. To test a sample's ability to hold water, punch a small hole in the bottom of a paper cup. Add soil until the cup is half full. Then pour 100 ml of water on top of the soil. Record the time it takes for the first drop of water to fall from the bottom of the cup (see Figure 7).

Color comparison is the most obvious similarity or difference between two samples. It can usually be made with the naked eye. Microscopic examination can reveal similarities or differences in the composition of two soils. Samples can be compared for plant matter, particle size, and artificial debris.

Punch hole with pencil in bottom of cup.

Fill cup ½ full of soil.

Add 100 ml of water to cup of soil. Time seconds passed before first drip.

Figure 7. Testing the water-holding ability of the soil.

Materials:

Soil sample from crime scene (Sample CS)
Soil sample from Sam's boots (Sample A)
Soil sample from Sam's tennis shoes (Sample B)
Soil sample from Sam's dress shoes (Sample C)

Answers to Conclusion Questions of Investigation 2–1:

1. Yes. Sample C and the crime scene were a match.

2. Soil evidence can be a valuable tool in linking a suspect to a crime scene. If the soil at a crime scene is unique to the area, it can be identified after it is transferred away from the crime. Almost anyone who is present at a crime scene affects the scene by picking up or leaving particles.

3. a. One way is by comparing the pH of each soil sample Acidity of soil can be determined in several ways. One simple test for soil pH is to add 100 ml of water to a small soil sample, stir, then pour the water and soil through a funnel lined with filter paper. The water collected below the funnel can be checked with pH paper.

   b. An investigator can also compare the water-holding capacities of two soil samples. To test a sample's ability to hold water, punch a small hole in the bottom of a paper cup. Add soil until the cup is half full. Then pour 100 ml of water on top of the soil. Record the amount of time it takes the water to collect below the cup.

   c. Microscopic examination can reveal similarities or differences in the composition of two soils. Samples can be compared for plant matter, particle size, and artificial debris. Color comparison is the most obvious similarity or difference between two samples.

4. Answers will vary.

NSTA *Objectives that apply to this investigation*

As a result of activities in grades K–4, all students should develop:

■ an understanding of properties of earth materials, objects in the sky, and changes in earth and sky. Students should understand fundamental concepts and principles that underlie the properties of earth materials. Earth's materials have different physical and chemical properties. (*Elementary Standard, Earth and Space Science*)

■ an understanding of properties of earth materials, objects in the sky, and changes in earth and sky. Students should understand fundamental concepts and principles that underlie the properties of earth materials. Students should understand soils have properties of color and texture, capacity to retain water, and ability to support the growth of many kinds of plants. (*Elementary Standard, Earth and Space Science*)

■ abilities of technological design, understanding about science and technology, and abilities to distinguish between natural objects and objects made by humans. Students should understand fundamental concepts and principles that underlie the understanding about science and technology. People have always had problems and invented tools and techniques to solve problems. Trying to determine the effects of solutions helps people avoid some new problems. (*Elementary Standard, Science and Technology*)

As a result of activities in grades 5–8, all students should develop:

■ abilities necessary to do scientific inquiry and understandings about scientific inquiry. Students should understand fundamental concepts and principles that underlie the understanding about the abilities necessary to do scientific inquiry. Students should design and conduct a scientific investigation. Students should develop general abilities, such as systematic observation, making accurate measurements, and identifying and controlling variables. (*Grades 5–8, Science as Inquiry*)

Name _____ Date _____

THE SOIL EVIDENCE
Student Investigator Page

The Crime

Mr. Sullivan always collects admission money at home football games. After halftime, he counts the money, locks it in a safe box, and places it in the trunk of his car. Then he joins his family for the last half of the game. Because the parking lot has not been paved, all cars at the game park in a field next to the ball field.

Friday night, Mr. Sullivan's trunk was pried open and the lock box was stolen. Police officers on the scene examined footprints around the car. They quickly determined that many prints belonged to Mr. Sullivan and his family. However, there was one set of large prints near the car that they could not identify.

Two witnesses claim they saw Sam Manley hanging around Mr. Sullivan's car after halftime. Police officers go to Sam's house Monday morning and ask to see all of his boots and shoes. They are looking for soil on his shoes that is like the soil from the crime scene. They scrape a little dirt off all of Sam's shoes. This soil is taken back to the forensic lab and compared to the soil from the crime scene.

Procedure

1. Write a hypothesis about the similarities or differences in soil at the crime scene and soil taken from Sam's shoes.

_____

_____

_____

_____

_____

_____

_____

_____

Use the scientific method to solve a problem.

A hypothesis states a problem or a question.

2. Develop an experiment to test your hypothesis. Write the procedure for your experiment in the space below.

_____

_____

_____

_____

_____

_____

3. List the materials you will need for your experiment.

_____

_____

_____

4. Show your experimental procedure and list of materials to your teacher. Get your teacher's approval before proceeding with your experiment.

Teacher's signature/approval_____

5. On another sheet of paper, create any Data Tables you need to record information from your experiment.

Conclusion Questions

1. Based on your experimental results, did the soil from any of Sam's shoes match the soil from the crime scene?

If soil at a crime scene is unique to an area, it can be used to identify the criminal.

_____

Which sample? _____

2. Why can soil be used as evidence in a crime?

_____

_____

_____

3. Describe three ways to compare soil samples.

_____

_____

_____

4. Write the end of this crime story.

_____

_____

_____

_____

_____

_____

_____

_____

INVESTIGATION 2–2
POINTING OUT POLLUTION

TEACHER INFORMATION

This investigation focuses on water pollution. To solve the problem of whether pollutants are entering a creek, students collect and evaluate data—pH of water samples along 8 collection sites.

Investigation Objectives:

Collect pH data on a hypothetical river.
Use this data to evaluate any sources of water pollution.

Time Required: 40 minutes

Notes for the Teacher:

1. Read the Background to students, then have them read The Crime.

2. Arrange students in groups of 2, 3, or 4. Give each group a copy of the Student Investigator Page and map (Figure 8). Photocopy Figure 9 from the Background or sketch it on the board for your students.

3. Review the concepts of pH and water quality. You might want to test the pH of several household items (see Figure 9) to be sure that students understand how to use hydronium paper. Hydronium paper can be purchased at any chemical supply company, and at many drug stores. If hydronium paper is not available, pH meters can also be used in this investigation.

4. To prepare the eight water samples, place tap water in eight large beakers. Label the beakers A–H. The water in beakers A–F represents normal creek water, so their values should be close to the following:

A—6.1	E—6.3
B—6.2	F—6.3
C—6.7	
D—6.3	

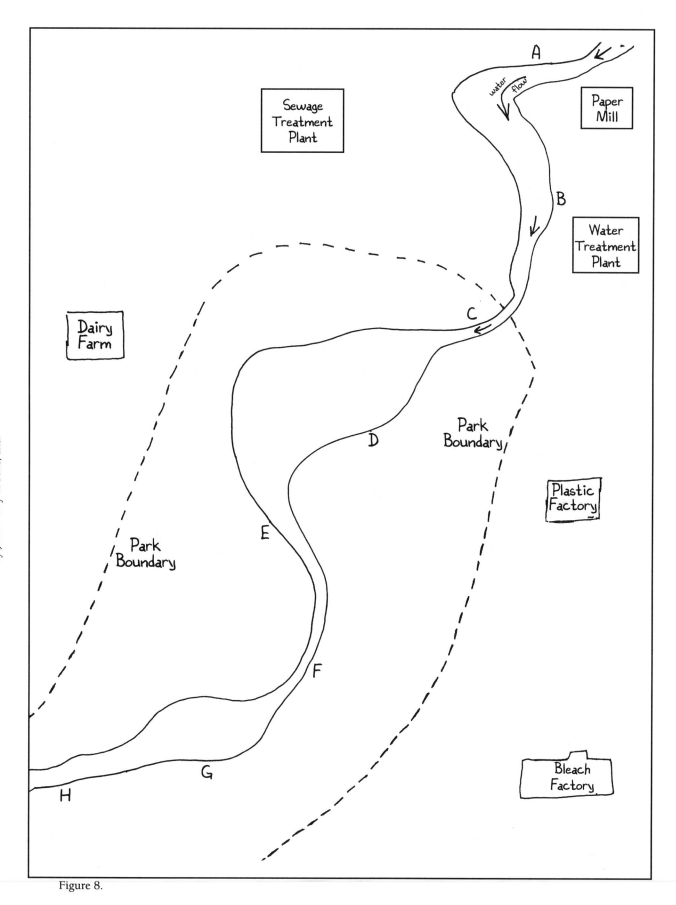

Figure 8.

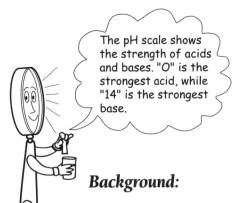

The pH scale shows the strength of acids and bases. "0" is the strongest acid, while "14" is the strongest base.

5. If you need to adjust the tap water, add a little acid (such as vinegar or dilute HCl) or a base (such as ammonia or dilute NaOH) as needed.

6. To prepare Sample G, add enough household ammonia or NaOH to tap water to bring the pH to 9.0. To prepare Sample H, add enough household ammonia or NaOH to the water to bring the pH to 8.0.

Background:

Water pollution is a serious problem. The water that presently exists on Earth is all of the water we will ever have. To keep this water usable, we must keep it clean.

There are two basic types of water pollution:

1. *Point-Source Pollution.* Pollution enters waterways from a pipe or some other clear point of discharge. For example, a sewer pipe from a home that empties into a river is an example of point-source pollution.

2. *Nonpoint-Source Pollution.* Pollution enters waterways from various sources, none of which can be clearly identified. Fertilizers, pesticides, and other chemicals that are washed off golf courses by rain into local creeks and rivers are good examples of this type of pollution.

Acids and bases are two kinds of water pollutants. Living things in waterways cannot survive in either a very acidic or a very basic environment. They prefer water that is neutral or nearly neutral.

Acidity and basicity are measured on a special scale called the pH scale. Numbers on the pH scale extend from 0 to 14. The most acidic substance known has a pH of 0. The most basic substance has a pH of 14. The value 7, which is right in the middle of the scale, is neither acidic nor basic. That is why pH 7 is described as "neutral."

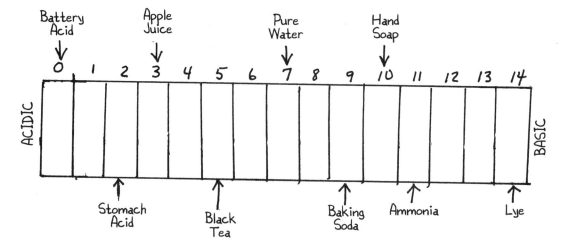

Figure 9. pH scale showing some common acids and bases.

You come in contact with acids and bases every day. Some mild acids include colas, fruit juices, and vinegar. Some mild bases are found in antacids and household cleaners. Strong bases are ingredients in drain cleaner and household ammonia. Some common acids and bases are arranged on the pH scale in Figure 9. Notice that pure water has a pH of 7.

Materials:

2 strips of pH (hydronium) paper
Key to pH paper
Bottom half of a petri dish
8 droppers
8 water samples
Paper
Tape
Scissors

Answers to Conclusion Questions of Investigation 2–2:

1. a. Point-source pollution enters a waterway from a pipe or some other point.

   b. Nonpoint-source pollution enters a waterway from various sources, none of which can be clearly identified.

2. 6.4

3. slightly acidic

4. Answers will vary, but a number greater than 7; most likely about 7.5.

5. slightly basic

6. Bleach factory. The only sites that showed abnormal pH values were downstream from the bleach factory.

7. Nonpoint source. There is no pipe or any other clear point of discharge entering the creek.

NSTA Objectives that apply to this investigation

As a result of activities in grades K–4, all students should develop:

- abilities necessary to do scientific inquiry and understanding about scientific inquiry. Students should employ simple equipment and tools to gather data and extend the senses. Students should use data to construct a reasonable explanation. (*Elementary Standard, Science as Inquiry*)

- understanding of personal health, characteristics and changes in population, types of resources, changes in environments, and science and technology in local challenges. Students should understand fundamental concepts and principles that underlie the understanding about changes in environments. Changes in environments can be natural or influenced by humans. Pollution is a change in the environment that can influence the health, survival, or activities of organisms, including humans. (*Elementary Standard, Science in Personal and Social Perspectives*)

■ understanding of personal health, characteristics and changes in population, types of resources, changes in environments, and science and technology in local challenges. Students should understand fundamental concepts and principles that underlie the understanding about science and technology in local challenges. People continue inventing new ways of doing things, solving problems, and getting work done. New ideas and inventions often affect other people; sometimes the effects are good and sometimes they are bad. It is helpful to try to determine in advance how ideas and inventions will affect other people. (*Elementary Standard, Science in Personal and Social Perspectives*)

As a result of activities in grades 5–8, all students should develop:

■ abilities necessary to do scientific inquiry and understandings about scientific inquiry. Students should use appropriate tools and techniques to gather, analyze, and interpret data. Students should develop descriptions, explanations, predictions, and models using evidence. Students should think critically and logically to make the relationships between evidence and explanations. (*Grades 5–8 Standard, Science as Inquiry*)

■ abilities necessary to do scientific inquiry and understandings about scientific inquiry. Students should understand fundamental concepts and principles that underlie the understanding about the abilities necessary to do scientific inquiry. Students should use appropriate tools and techniques to gather, analyze, and interpret data. (*Grades 5–8, Science as Inquiry*)

■ abilities necessary to do scientific inquiry and understandings about scientific inquiry. Students should understand fundamental concepts and principles that underlie the understanding about the abilities necessary to do scientific inquiry. Students should design and conduct a scientific investigation. Students should develop general abilities, such as systematic observation, making accurate measurements, and identifying and controlling variables. (*Grades 5–8, Science as Inquiry*)

■ abilities necessary to do scientific inquiry and understandings about scientific inquiry. Students should understand fundamental concepts and principles that underlie the understanding about the abilities necessary to do scientific inquiry. Students should recognize and analyze alternative explanations and predictions. Students should develop the ability to listen to and respect the explanations proposed by other students. (*Grades 5–8, Science as Inquiry*)

■ understanding of structure of the earth system, Earth's history, and Earth in the solar system. Students should understand fundamental concepts and principles that underlie the understanding of risks and benefits. Students should understand the risks associated with natural hazards (fires, floods, and tornadoes), with chemical hazards (pollutants in air, water, soil, and food), with biological hazards (pollen, viruses, bacterial, and parasites), social hazards, and personal hazards. (*Grades 5–8 Standard, Earth and Space Science*)

Name _____ Date _____

POINTING OUT POLLUTION
Student Investigator Page

The Crime

The city of Crystal made a rule to preserve the natural beauty of Crystal Creek. This creek begins in a nearby mountain, flows through Crystal and several other small towns, and eventually joins a river. Much of the land next to the creek was set aside as a park to give the creek some additional protection. Everyone who lives or works along the creek has been notified to keep it clean. Anyone who pollutes the creek will have to pay a fine.

Even though there are no sewer pipes entering the creek, park officials have recently noticed some signs of water pollution. Several dead fish have floated to the surface. Many of the creek plants have turned brown and died. There is some concern that pollutants are entering the creek. Park officials have asked the Crystal water quality technicians to collect water samples from their eight collection points and check them for pollution. The technicians can then compare their findings with information they recorded six months ago. (See Data Table 1). At that time, the pH of the water was considered to be "normal." To see the collection points, see the map.

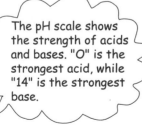

The pH scale shows the strength of acids and bases. "O" is the strongest acid, while "14" is the strongest base.

DATA TABLE 1. pH OF WATER SAMPLES ALONG 8 COLLECTION SITES (6 MONTHS AGO).	
Sampling Site	*pH*
A	6.1
B	6.2
C	6.7
D	6.3
E	6.3
F	6.5
G	6.8
H	6.5

Procedure

1. Cut a piece of paper into a circle about the size of a quarter.

2. Tape the circle in the middle of your petri dish.

3. Label the circle as shown in Figure 10.

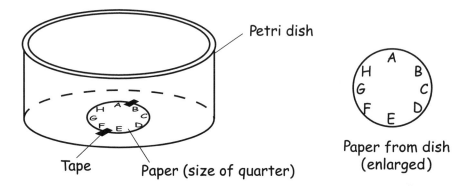

Figure 10. Cut a piece of paper into a small circle, and tape it in the center of the petri dish. Label it with the letters A–H.

4. Tear each piece of pH paper into four parts.

5. Position the pH paper parts around the small circle in the petri dish so that one piece corresponds to one letter (see Figure 11).

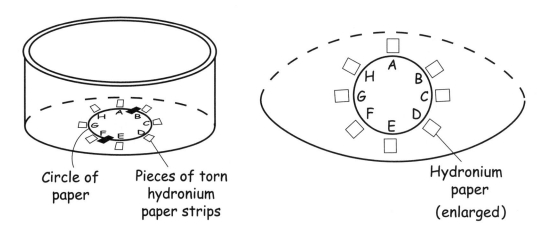

Figure 11. Arrange the pieces of hydronium paper so that each piece corresponds to one letter.

6. With a dropper, place 2 or 3 drops of water from location A on the piece of pH paper labeled A. Note any color change. Using the key to the pH paper as a guide, determine the pH shown on your hydronium paper. Record the color of the paper and the pH of the water sample in Data Table 2. Also indicate whether this sample was acidic or basic.

7. Repeat the same procedure with the other 7 water samples.

DATA TABLE 2. WATER SAMPLES, COLOR OF PH PAPER, AND PH.			
Sample	**Color of pH paper**	**pH**	**Acid or Base?**
A			
B			
C			
D			
E			
F			
G			
H			

Conclusion Questions

1. Name and describe two types of water pollution.

   _____

   _____

   _____

   _____

2. Based on the information in Data Table 1, what was the average pH of Crystal Creek 6 months ago? (Determine the average by adding together all of the pH values, then dividing by 8.)

   _____

   _____

   _____

3. Based on the information in Data Table 1, would you say that the water in a creek is normally: slightly acidic, neutral, or slightly basic?

   _____

   _____

   _____

4. Based on the information you supplied in Data Table 2, what is the average pH of Crystal Creek now?

_____

_____

_____

5. Is the pollution entering Crystal Creek acidic or basic?

_____

_____

_____

6. Based on your results, where do you think the water pollution in Crystal Creek is coming from: the paper mill, water treatment plant, sewage treatment plant, dairy farm, plastic factory, or bleach factory? Explain your answer.

_____

_____

_____

_____

7. What type of pollution is entering Crystal Creek: point-source or nonpoint-source pollution? Why?

_____

_____

_____

_____

_____

INVESTIGATION 2–3
DIRTY CLUES

TEACHER INFORMATION

Students investigate whether a farmer's soil that was supposed to be treated with nitrogen and phosphorous was actually treated. They collect soil at different depths and compare the samples to solve the crime.

Investigation Objective:

Compare the amounts of nitrogen and phosphorus in two soil samples.

Time Required: 50 minutes

Notes for the Teacher:

1. Read the Background to students, then have them read The Crime.

2. Copy the Student Investigator Page for each student or for each group of students. This activity is best done in groups of 2 or 3 students.

3. Buy kits that can be used to test soil nutrient levels and pH, such as the Sudbury® Soil Test Kit. These are available at most home and garden stores. All chemicals and equipment needed for testing are enclosed in the kit. Some kits may test for more minerals than we will check in this investigation; feel free to extend the lesson by testing for these additional nutrients.

4. Collect a few cups of soil from a depth of two to three inches. Divide the soil into two containers.

5. Label one container "T" and the other "F."

Nitrogen and phosphorus are two important soil nutrients.

Background:

Soil is the material that holds and supports plants. It contains all of the nutrients that plants need. Animals take in these nutrients by eating plants. When plants and animals die, the nutrients in their bodies return to the soil.

Soil is a difficult item to define for two reasons:

  a. It is made up of a wide variety of materials.

  b. It plays a lot of different roles in nature.

   For example, much of soil is made of weathered rock, a nonliving substance. Yet, many types of soil contain as much living material as nonliving. Tiny animals, plants, and fungi as well as one-celled organisms live within the soil.
   Some of the nutrients found in soil are nitrogen, phosphorus, calcium, magnesium, sulfur, iron, potassium, chlorine, manganese, copper, and zinc. These are also the nutrients needed for plant growth; nitrogen and phosphorus are two of the most important.
   Plants need nitrogen for dark green stems and leaves. Plants lacking nitrogen have a sickly, yellow-green color. They grow so slowly that they have a distinctive dwarfed or stunted look. Their leaves become dry and brittle.
   Phosphorus is required for healthy growth of flowers, seeds, and grains. When plants don't get enough phosphorus, their leaves, stems, and branches have a purplish color. They grow slowly and produce few flowers, fruits, and grains.

Materials:

Soil sample from terrarium (T)
Soil sample from field (F)
Soil test kit

Answers to Conclusion Questions of Investigation 2–3:

  1. Soil holds and supports plants. It contains all of the nutrients that plants need. Much of soil is made of weathered rock, a nonliving substance. Yet, many types of soil contain as much living material as nonliving. Tiny animals, plants, and fungi as well as one-celled organisms live within the soil.

  2. Answers may include any five of the following: nitrogen, phosphorus, calcium, magnesium, sulfur, iron, potassium, chlorine, manganese, copper, and zinc.

  3. Plants need nitrogen for dark green stems and leaves. Plants lacking nitrogen have a sickly, yellow-green color. They grow slowly, giving a dwarfed or stunted look. Their leaves turn dry, starting with those near the ground and moving up the plant. Phosphorus is required for healthy growth of flowers, seeds, and grains. When plants don't get enough phosphorus, their leaves, stems, and branches have a purplish color. They grow slowly and produce few flowers, fruits, and grains.

  4. They are the same.

  5. Answers may vary, but most will say "No."

  6. a. 52 cm

      b. 74 cm

      c. increased levels of nitrogen cause an increase in plant height

    d. 1996; increased plant height

    e. it has gradually decreased; answers may vary, but they might suggest erosion or uptake by plants

NSTA Objectives that apply to this investigation

As a result of activities in grades K–4, all students should develop:

- an understanding of properties of earth materials, objects in the sky, and changes in earth and sky. Students should understand fundamental concepts and principles that underlie the properties of earth materials. Earth's materials have different physical and chemical properties. (*Elementary Standard, Earth and Space Science*)

- an understanding of properties of earth materials, objects in the sky, and changes in earth and sky. Students should understand fundamental concepts and principles that underlie the properties of earth materials. Students should understand soils have properties of color and texture, capacity to retain water, and ability to support the growth of many kinds of plants. (*Elementary Standard, Earth and Space Science*)

As a result of activities in grades 5–8, all students should develop:

- abilities necessary to do scientific inquiry and understandings about scientific inquiry. Students should use appropriate tools and techniques to gather, analyze, and interpret data. Students should think critically and logically to make the relationships between evidence and explanations. (*Grades 5–8 Standard, Science as Inquiry*)

- abilities necessary to do scientific inquiry and understandings about scientific inquiry. Students should understand fundamental concepts and principles that underlie the understanding about the abilities necessary to do scientific inquiry. Students should think critically and logically to make the relationships between evidence and explanations. Students should be able to review data from a simple experiment, summarize the data, and form a logical argument about the cause-and-effect relationships in the experiment. (*Grades 5–8 Standard, Science as Inquiry*)

- abilities necessary to do scientific inquiry and understandings about scientific inquiry. Students should understand fundamental concepts and principles that underlie the understanding about the abilities necessary to do scientific inquiry. Students should use appropriate tools and techniques to gather, analyze, and interpret data. (*Grades 5–8, Science as Inquiry*)

- understanding of structure of the earth system, Earth's history, and Earth in the solar system. Students should understand fundamental concepts and principles that underlie the understanding of the structure of the Earth system. Soil consists of weathered rocks and decomposed organic material from dead plants, animals, and bacteria. Soils are often found in layers, with each having a different chemical composition and texture. (*Grades 5–8 Standard, Earth Science*)

Name _____ Date _____

DIRTY CLUES
Student Investigator Page

The Crime

Mr. Rex is reading the evening paper when an advertisement catches his attention.

> Call Dirt Doctor
> if your soil is weak,
> your plants are skinny,
> and your flowers are puny.
> Dirt Doctor will fix
> your soil.
> Don't delay! Call today.
> 1-800-DIRTDOC

This year has not been a good one on Mr. Rex's farm. He is afraid that the quality of his soil is not so good as it used to be. Mr. Rex and his family have owned the land he farms for 150 years, and until this year they've had healthy crops.

The next day, Mr. Rex calls the Dirt Doctor and asks him to check the levels of nutrients in his soil. Just as Mr. Rex feared, Dirt Doctor tells him that his nitrogen and phosphorus levels are very low. According to the Doc, a lack of these two nutrients is causing Mr. Rex's problems. He encourages Mr. Rex to have his soil treated, and Mr. Rex agrees to do so. Mr. Rex pays Dirt Doctor $5,000 for the treatment.

A year passes, and Mr. Rex is evaluating his crops once again. He is very disappointed because this year has not been any better than last. Considering the high cost of soil treatment, he feels that the Dirt Doctor may have cheated him. If the soil had been treated, why weren't the crops better?

Mr. Rex calls the local police and lodges a complaint against the Dirt Doctor. He wants his money back. The police ask their soil scientist, Sandy Loam, to visit Mr. Rex's farm and check the soil.

> Nitrogen and phosphorus are two important soil nutrients.

When Sandy arrives, she walks over the fields and examines a few dying plants. Mr. Rex, his wife Susan, and daughter Sarah stand in the front yard and watch her. When she's finished, Sandy asks the Rex family if they have any dirt from their farm that was not treated by the Dirt Doctor. While her parents are thinking, Sarah reminds everyone that she's had her terrarium for more than a year, and it contains soil from the farm.

Sandy takes a few grams of soil from the terrarium and pours it into a test tube labeled "T." On the way back to the lab, she stops at the field and gathers a few grams of soil. She places these in a test tube labeled "F." Sandy continues to her lab with the two samples.

Procedure

1. Open the instruction book in the soil test kit and find the page that explains the nitrogen (N) test.

2. Read the directions for conducting the nitrogen test. As you are reading, write down the materials you will need from the kit for this test.

3. Following the instructions for this test, check the terrarium (T) soil sample for nitrogen.

4. Record the amount of nitrogen in the terrarium soil in Data Table 1. Clean the test kit equipment.

5. Repeat steps 3 and 4 with the field (F) soil sample.

6. Find the page in the instruction book that explains the phosphorus (P) test.

7. Read the directions for conducting the phosphorus test. As you are reading, write down the materials you will need from the kit for this test.

8. Follow the instructions for completing the phosphorus test on the terrarium soil sample.

9. Record the amount of phosphorus in the terrarium soil in Data Table 1. Clean the test equipment.

10. Repeat steps 8 and 9 for the field soil sample.

DATA TABLE 1. LEVELS OF NITROGEN AND PHOSPHORUS IN TWO SOIL SAMPLES.		
Soil samples	**Nitrogen (N) levels**	**Phosphorus (P) levels**
Terrarium (T)		
Field (F)		

Conclusion Questions

1. Define or describe soil.

_____

_____

_____

2. List five of the plant nutrients found in soil.

   _____

   _____

   _____

3. Why do plants need nitrogen? Why do they need phosphorus?

   _____

   _____

   _____

4. How did the nitrogen and phosphorus levels in these two soil samples compare?

   _____

   _____

   _____

5. In your opinion, did the Dirt Doctor treat Mr. Rex's fields with nitrogen and phosphorus?

   _____

6. Examine Data Table 2, and then answer these questions:

   a. What was the height of the corn plants when nitrogen levels reached their lowest point?

   _____

   b. What was the height of corn plants when nitrogen levels reached their highest point?

   _____

   c. Based on the information in this graph, how do nitrogen levels affect the growth of plants?

   _____

   d. One year Mr. Rex added chicken manure to his fields. Chicken manure, like all types of animal feces, contains a lot of nitrogen. Based on the graph, in what year did Mr. Rex use the manure? How did it affect plant growth?

   _____

   _____

   _____

   e. What happened to the levels of nitrogen on Mr. Rex's farm from 1990 to 1995? In your opinion, what might have caused this change?

   _____

   _____

   _____

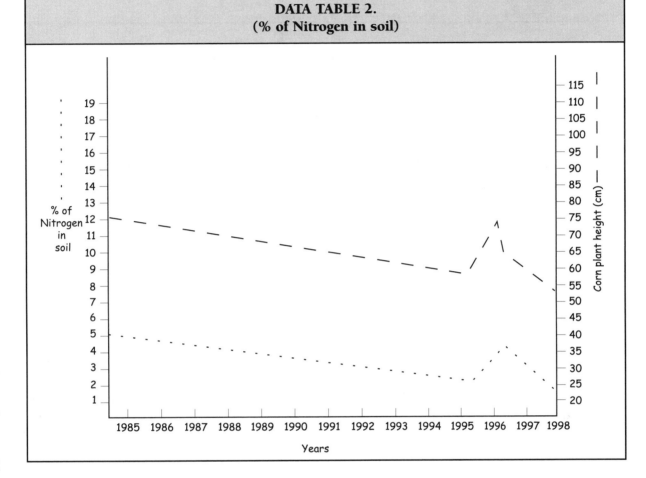

DATA TABLE 2.
(% of Nitrogen in soil)

INVESTIGATION 2–4

DIRTY DAVE

TEACHER INFORMATION

To conduct this investigation, students compare soil samples from the crime scene to samples taken from the suspect's pants, along with other samples from where the suspect claims to have been. Students examine the texture as well as the natural and man-made components of the soil samples under a microscope.

Investigation Objective:

Compare characteristics of soil samples taken from different locations.

Time Required: 50 minutes

Notes for the Teacher:

1. Read the Background to students, then have them read The Crime.

2. Copy the Student Investigator Page for each student or for each group of students. This activity is best done in groups of 2 or 3 students.

> Crime scene investigators look at both natural and man-made objects when they inspect the soil.

3. Several days before the investigation, collect six soil samples from six locations. Try to make the samples as different as possible in type, amount of plant debris, and color. Only the top two inches of the soil should be collected. Place the soil samples in self-locking bags and mark each sample with one of the following labels: *1. The park*; *2. The mall*; *3. Dave's yard*; *4. Jeff's yard*; *5. Beside highway I–20*; *6. Josh's worksite*. Collect an extra bag of soil from the location you designate as Josh's worksite and label it: *7. Dave's pants*.

4. While at Josh's worksite location, take an old pair of pants and rub them across the ground so a dirt stain is evident on the pants.

5. Obtain some paint chips from an old house or other structure where paint is peeling. Crumble some of these paint chips into "Josh's worksite" sample and mix it thoroughly with the soil. Do the same for the soil sample marked "Dave's pants." sample.

6. For the next 24–48 hours, leave the bags open and allow the soils to air dry. The morning of the investigation, place these bags and the stained piece of clothing on the table for the students. At the beginning of the investigation, tell students that the stained clothing was taken from the suspect and the dirt from it was scraped into the bag marked "Dave's pants." Also tell the class the other six soil samples were taken from various locations around town where the suspect may have stained his clothing. Students should determine if the soil sample from "Dave's pants" matches any of the six samples provided.

Background:

Science defines soil as material on or near the Earth's surface. When crime scene investigators analyze soil samples, they look at many things in the soil. They inspect the soil for both natural and man-made objects. Natural objects include rocks, minerals, and plants in the soil. Glass, cinders, paint chips, and metals are some man-made objects they may find in the soil samples. The presence of these objects may help to match soil taken from a suspect with the scene of a crime. This establishes a link between the suspect and the crime.

Soil evidence must be carefully transported from the scene of a crime to the lab. Once soil samples are taken to the lab, they are dried in an oven. This prevents the presence of moisture from interfering with color analysis of the soil.

There are several aspects of soil that experts identify. The first is soil color. Then soil samples are examined under low power of a microscope for evidence of natural and man-made items. The examiner makes notes about all materials he or she finds in each sample. The different sizes of particles are noted (Figure 12), as well as the texture of the particles.

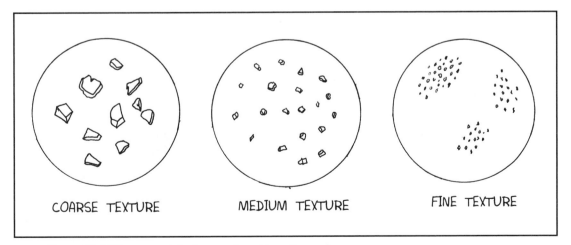

Figure 12. Different particle sizes are found in soil samples.

Materials:

7 plastic bags of soil
Tape
Crayons
Stereo microscope or magnifying glass
Clear plastic cups
Spoon
Masking tape
Black marker
7 pieces of white paper

Answers to Conclusion Questions of Investigation 2–4:

1. yes

2. Answers will vary; but no, the evidence only shows that Dave was present at Josh's worksite.

3. color, natural and man-made objects in soil, and shape of particles

4. paint chips

5. Answers will vary.

NSTA Objectives that apply to this investigation

As a result of activities in grades K–4, all students should develop:

■ abilities necessary to do scientific inquiry and understanding about scientific inquiry. Students should employ simple equipment and tools to gather data and extend the senses. Students should use data to construct a reasonable explanation. (*Elementary Standard, Science as Inquiry*)

■ an understanding of properties of earth materials, objects in the sky, and changes in earth and sky. Students should understand fundamental concepts and principles that underlie the properties of earth materials. Students should understand soils have properties of color and texture, capacity to retain water, and ability to support the growth of many kinds of plants. (*Elementary Standard, Earth and Space Science*)

As a result of activities in grades 5–8, all students should develop:

■ abilities necessary to do scientific inquiry and understandings about scientific inquiry. Students should use appropriate tools and techniques to gather, analyze, and interpret data. Students should think critically and logically to make the relationships between evidence and explanations. (*Grades 5–8 Standard, Science as Inquiry*)

■ abilities necessary to do scientific inquiry and understandings about scientific inquiry. Students should understand fundamental concepts and principles that underlie the understanding about the abilities necessary to do scientific inquiry. Students should think critically and logically to make the relationships between evidence and explanations. Students should be able to review data from a simple experiment, summarize the data, and form a logical argument about the cause-and-effect relationships in the experiment. (*Grades 5–8 Standard, Science as Inquiry*)

■ abilities necessary to do scientific inquiry and understanding about scientific inquiry. Students should understand fundamental concepts and principles that underlie the understanding about the abilities necessary to do scientific inquiry. Students should design and conduct a scientific investigation. Students should develop general abilities, such as systematic observation, making accurate measurements, and identifying and controlling variables. (*Grades 5–8, Science as Inquiry*)

■ understanding of structure of the earth system, Earth's history, and Earth in the solar system. Students should understand fundamental concepts and principles that underlie the understanding of the structure of the Earth system. Soil consists of weathered rocks and decomposed organic material from dead plants, animals, and bacteria. Soils are often found in layers, with each having a different chemical composition and texture. (*Grades 5–8 Standard, Earth Science*)

Name _____ Date _____

DIRTY DAVE
Student Investigator Page

The Crime

Josh Kline is in the hospital with a broken leg. Josh is a painter. Saturday afternoon he was working at a job site where he was scraping old paint from a house. The rest of his crew had left for the day. Near dark, the ladder he was standing on began to tip backward. As he fell Josh saw a masked man on the ground pushing his ladder. When Josh hit the ground, his right leg broke. While he was lying there, the masked man bent down on his knees beside Josh and took Josh's wallet. Before the masked man could flee, Josh tripped him. As he stumbled and fell, Josh noticed that the masked man had the same build and haircut as his next door neighbor, Dave Hale. Josh could not reach the masked man, and his assailant scrambled to his feet and escaped.

Josh crawled to his cellular phone and dialed 911. Police officers arrived, took a statement from Josh, and sent him to the hospital. Investigators took a sample of soil from the place where the masked man fell when he was tripped by Josh. They also visited Dave Hale. He was not home, but they found him at a park near his house. Dave had on khaki pants that had a huge dirt stain across the front. Dave could not remember where he got the stain, but offered five different suggestions:

- Near the stream at the park, where he lay on his stomach to watch the fish swim.
- Outside the mall, where he slipped on an ice cream cone and fell in the flower bed.
- At home, where he crawled under the house to get his cat.
- At his friend Jeff's house, where he stopped to help Jeff repair his sewage system.
- Along the side of highway I–20, where he helped a lady change a flat tire.

Dave led investigators to all of these locations and they took soil samples from each.

Police officers escorted Dave home and asked him to change clothes. They took his dirty khaki pants to the lab. Dirt was collected from Dave's pants and bagged as evidence.

You can help solve this crime by comparing the soil samples from Dave's pants with soil taken from different locations. You can determine whether the stain on Dave's pants came from one of the locations he visited today or if it came from Josh's worksite.

Procedure

1. Use masking tape and a black marker to label seven plastic cups as follows:

The park   The mall

Dave's yard   Jeff's yard

Beside highway I–20   Josh's worksite

Dave's pants

> Crime scene investigators look at both natural and man-made objects when they inspect the soil.

2. Place the same labels on the seven pieces of white paper.

3. Carefully pour the soil samples from the cups onto the appropriate pieces of white paper. Observe the different colors and record your observations in the column labeled "Color of sample" on the Data Table.

4. Look through the samples and search for any evidence of natural or man-made debris, such as plants, sticks, metals, paint chips, fabrics, etc. Record any evidence you see in the Data Table under "Man-made or natural material."

DATA TABLE. DESCRIPTION OF SOIL SAMPLES.			
	Color of sample	*Man-made or natural material*	*Drawing of particles*
The park			
The mall			
Dave's yard			
Jeff's yard			
Beside Highway I-20			
Josh's worksite			
Dave's pants			

5. With the sticky side of a small piece of clear tape, gather a thin layer of soil from one of the soil samples. Place this under the stereo microscope or your magnifying glass. In the column labeled "Drawing of particles," draw the different sizes of particles and color them appropriately. Be sure to record any unusual items you see under the microscope. Repeat this procedure for all seven samples.

6. Look at the Data Table and decide if any of the samples match the sample from Dave's pants.

Conclusion Questions

1. Did your results indicate that Dave was at Josh's worksite on the day of the crime?

   _____

   _____

2. If the answer to question 1 was yes, do you think that is enough evidence to convict Dave of the crime? Explain your answer.

   _____

   _____

   _____

   _____

   _____

3. Name the soil characteristics you studied in this lab.

   _____

   _____

4. What one piece of evidence in the soil sample helped you match the sample from Dave's pants to the location from which Dave obtained the stain?

   _____

   _____

5. Write a conclusion to this crime. In your ending describe how you would present to the jury the argument for or against Dave.

   _____

   _____

   _____

   _____

   _____

   _____

INVESTIGATION 2–5

THE SAND-TRAP BLUES

TEACHER INFORMATION

When sand traps recently repaired at a local golf course don't allow drainage, students determine whether the traps were repaired with high-quality sand as required or with other materials. To do this, they test how long it takes for water to drain through materials such as sand, silt, and clay.

Investigation Objective:

Determine if an unknown soil sample is pure sand or a mixture of sand and other substances.

Time Required: 50 minutes

Notes for the Teacher:

1. Read the Background to students, then have them read The Crime.

2. Copy the Student Investigator Page for each student or for each group of students. Draw the appearance of the soil particles on the board (Figure 13) prior to reading the Background to your students. This activity is best done in groups of 2 or 3 students.

3. Prior to the investigation, collect about 500 grams of the following soil samples:

    pure sand (sample 1)

    topsoil, loam, or silt (sample 2)

    clay (sample 3)

    Label each sample with its appropriate name.

4. Also prior to the investigation, prepare the following samples and label them with the appropriate letter:

    Bag A—place pure sand

    Bag B—prepare a mixture of sand, clay, and topsoil

    Bag C—prepare a mixture of a little sand mixed with a great deal of clay

5. When gathering the supplies for this investigation, choose Styrofoam cups that can be suspended in a clear plastic cup without touching the bottom of the plastic cup.

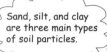

6. Make sure each group has access to a clock or watch with a second hand.

Background:

Soil is a mixture of very small rocks, mineral particles, living organisms, air, and water. Some characteristics of the soil are due to the size of the particles. There are three main types of soil particles: sand, silt, and clay (Figure 13). Sandy soil has a coarse texture and consists of large particles. Silty soil is made of smaller particles and, consequently, its texture is not so coarse as sand's. Clay soil is made of small particles that have a fine texture. Topsoil or loam is a mixture of more than one type of soil.

The texture of the soil affects the speed of water moving through it. Sand and its large particles allow water to travel through quickly. Clay soil with its small particles does not allow water to move easily through it. Flooding can occur in areas where water will not move quickly into the earth. Silty soils are intermediate between clay and sand.

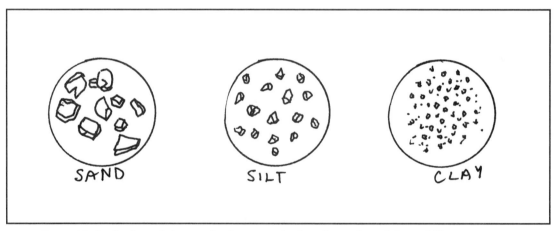

Figure 13. Sand, silt, and clay are the three particles found in soil. Each has a different texture.

Materials:

3 Styrofoam cups
Pencil
Cotton
Ruler
Masking tape
Water
Sand (about 500 grams)

Clay (about 500 grams)
Silt (about 500 grams)
Graduated cylinder
3 clear plastic cups (smaller in size than the Styrofoam cups)
Watch with a second hand
Sand trap soil samples A, B, and C

Answers to Conclusion Questions of Investigation 2–5:

1. sand; clay

2. No. Water did not penetrate all of them so quickly as it did through sand.

3. Yes. Water passed through the sand samples too slowly for the samples to be pure sand.

4. No. Water drains through sand very quickly.

5. Answers will vary; they might suggest that Casper was trying to save money.

NSTA Objectives that apply to this investigation

As a result of activities in grades K–4, all students should develop:

■ abilities necessary to do scientific inquiry and understanding about scientific inquiry. Students should employ simple equipment and tools to gather data and extend the senses. Students should use data to construct a reasonable explanation. (*Elementary Standard, Science as Inquiry*)

■ an understanding of properties of earth materials, objects in the sky, and changes in earth and sky. Students should understand fundamental concepts and principles that underlie the properties of earth materials. Earth's materials have different physical and chemical properties. (*Elementary Standard, Earth and Space Science*)

■ an understanding of properties of earth materials, objects in the sky, and changes in earth and sky. Students should understand fundamental concepts and principles that underlie the properties of earth materials. Students should understand soils have properties of color and texture, capacity to retain water, and ability to support the growth of many kinds of plants. (*Elementary Standard, Earth and Space Science*)

■ abilities necessary to do scientific inquiry and understanding about scientific inquiry. Students should use data to construct a reasonable explanation. (*Elementary Standard, Science as Inquiry*)

As a result of activities in grades 5–8, all students should develop:

■ abilities necessary to do scientific inquiry and understandings about scientific inquiry. Students should use appropriate tools and techniques to gather, analyze, and interpret data. Students should think critically and logically to make the relationships between evidence and explanations. (*Grades 5–8 Standard, Science as Inquiry*)

■ abilities necessary to do scientific inquiry and understandings about scientific inquiry. Students should understand fundamental concepts and principles that underlie the understanding about the abilities necessary to do scientific inquiry. Students should think critically and logically to make the relationships between evidence and explanations. Students should be able to review data from a simple experiment, summarize the data, and form a logical argument about the cause-and-effect relationships in the experiment. (*Grades 5–8 Standard, Science as Inquiry*)

■ abilities necessary to do scientific inquiry and understandings about scientific inquiry. Students should understand fundamental concepts and principles that underlie the understanding about the abilities necessary to do scientific inquiry. Students should develop descriptions, explanations, predictions, and models using evidence. (*Grades 5–8, Science as Inquiry*)

■ abilities necessary to do scientific inquiry and understandings about scientific inquiry. Students should understand fundamental concepts and principles that underlie the understanding about the abilities necessary to do scientific inquiry. Students should use appropriate tools and techniques to gather, analyze, and interpret data. (*Grades 5–8, Science as Inquiry*)

■ understanding of structure of the earth system, Earth's history, and Earth in the solar system. Students should understand fundamental concepts and principles that underlie the understanding of the structure of the Earth system. Soil consists of weathered rocks and decomposed organic material from dead plants, animals, and bacteria. Soils are often found in layers, with each having a different chemical composition and texture. (*Grades 5–8 Standard, Earth Science*)

Name _____ Date _____

THE SAND-TRAP BLUES
Student Investigator Page

The Crime

Belview Golf Club is one of the oldest golf courses in the United States. This year the owner, Ms. Mickey Barber, decided it was time to make some improvements. Members of the golf club completed a survey describing the things they would like to see improved about the course. Results of the survey indicated the sand traps were in immediate need of attention.

Mickey collected sand-trap repair cost estimates from several local golf course maintenance companies. Casper Schuler, the owner of Baywatch, was awarded the job at Belview. The contract Casper signed with Mickey directed he scrape each sand trap, haul in and fill each sand trap with high-quality sand, and smooth and level the sand. Mickey reviewed the terms of the contract carefully with Casper. Mickey was astonished at Casper's low prices because high-quality sand was very expensive.

Three weeks later Casper collected his fee when he finished the last sand trap at Belview. Everyone agreed the sand traps looked beautiful. A few days after Casper's job was finished, it rained heavily in the area. After the rain, standing water was found in all the sand traps. No drainage had occurred and Mickey's ground crew had to scoop water from the traps to make them playable again. Mickey tried telephoning Casper to inquire about this disaster. She was unable to reach him. It rained for the next several days and the problem of standing water happened each time.

Mickey finally went to Casper's place of business to confront him about the sand-trap dilemma. Casper told her he had followed their contract exactly and it was not his problem. Mickey suspected Casper may not have used pure sand to refill the traps after scraping them, so she hired a team of earth scientists to come in and conduct some tests.

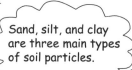

Sand, silt, and clay are three main types of soil particles.

The team of scientists arrived and collected samples from various sand traps. They collected samples from each sand trap at different depths. If the sand was mixed with other materials, the scientists would be able to determine this. Scientists brought in known samples of sand, clay, and silt. To establish baseline data, they conducted tests to determine how long it took for water to drain through each of these three types. After recording this data, they tested the samples from various depths in the sand trap for water penetration. A comparison of these results would determine if Casper used pure sand to fill the traps.

Procedure

Part A: Water drainage of sand, silt, and clay

1. Use a pencil to make five holes in the bottom of each Styrofoam cup.

2. Use your ruler and measure from the bottom of each cup up to the 6-cm mark. Use your pencil or a pen to make a mark on each cup at the 6-cm point (Figure 14).

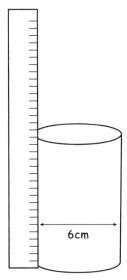

Figure 14. Measuring the Styrofoam cup with the ruler.

3. Place a thin layer of cotton in the bottom of all three cups.

4. Label the three cups: 1, 2, and 3.

5. Fill each cup with the appropriate sample up to the 6-cm mark:

   Cup 1—Sand

   Cup 2—Silt

   Cup 3—Clay

6. Place each Styrofoam cup so it is suspended in a clear plastic cup. The Styrofoam cups should be positioned so they do not touch the bottom of the plastic cup.

7. Add 100 ml of water to each Styrofoam cup, noting what time you added the water to each cup. Record in Data Table 1 how many seconds it took for the first drop of water to drip from each Styrofoam cup into the plastic cup below.

8. Allow the water to drip into the plastic cups for 10 minutes. Remove the Styrofoam cups and pour the amount of water collected in each plastic cup into a graduated cylinder. In Data Table 1 record how much water collected in each plastic cup.

9. Discard the contents of each Styrofoam cup. Pour the water from the graduated cylinders down the drain. Wash and dry the plastic cups and Styrofoam cups.

Part B: Water drainage of three soil samples from the sand traps

1. Repeat steps 1–9, but instead of using sand, silt, and clay, place Unknown Soil Sample A in cup 1, Unknown Soil Sample B in Cup 2, and Unknown Soil Sample C in Cup 3. Sample A was collected from the top of the sand traps; sample B, a few inches deep in the sand trap; and sample C, at least 8 inches deep in the sand trap.

2. Record your results from steps 7 and 8 from Part A in Data Table 2.

DATA TABLE 1. WATER DRAINAGE OF SAND, SILT, AND CLAY.		
	Number of seconds for first water drop to fall	*Milliliters of water in plastic cup after 10 minutes*
Sand: Sample 1		
Silt: Sample 2		
Clay: Sample 3		

DATA TABLE 2. WATER DRAINAGE OF THREE SOIL SAMPLES FROM THE SAND TRAPS.		
	Number of seconds for first water drop to fall	*Milliliters of water in plastic cup after 10 minutes*
Soil sample A		
Soil sample B		
Soil sample C		

Conclusion Questions

1. Refer to Data Table 1. Through which of the three soil types did water penetrate the quickest? Through which type did water penetrate the slowest?

   _____

   _____

   _____

2. Do you think all the samples from the sand trap were pure sand? Explain your answer.

   _____

   _____

   _____

   _____

   _____

3. Do you think Casper violated his contract? Explain your reason.

   _____

   _____

   _____

   _____

   _____

4. If the sand traps had been filled with pure sand, would water be likely to stand in it after a hard rain? Why or why not?

   _____

   _____

   _____

   _____

5. If you believe Casper did not fill the sand trap with pure sand, offer why he may have mixed something in with the pure sand when filling the trap.

   _____

   _____

   _____

   _____

   _____

INVESTIGATION 2–6

DIGGING UP CLUES

TEACHER INFORMATION

Who stole a car and left it at a landscaping worksite? Students compare soil samples from the car's tires to samples from various locations and from landscapers' boots. By observing soil components under a microscope, they determine the location of the samples and solve the crime.

Investigation Objective:

Observe several soil samples, describe them, and decide if two came from the same location.

Time Required: 50 minutes

Notes for the Teacher:

1. Read the Background to students, then have them read The Crime.

2. Copy the Student Investigator Page for each student or for each group of students. This activity is best done in groups of 2 or 3 students.

3. Collect 5 different soil samples. Divide one of the samples into two parts: Label one part "Sample CS" and the other part "Sample A." Label the remaining samples as: "Sample B," "Sample C," "Sample D," and "Sample E."

Soil can provide a link between the crime scene and the suspect.

Background:

Soil can serve as valuable evidence in a criminal case. Soil at a crime scene can be moved to other locations on a person's clothing or on a car. That is why soil can provide a link between a crime scene and a suspect.

Side-by-side visual examination of color is the first step in comparing two soil samples. There are more than 1,000 colors of soil. Color comparison should always be done on dry samples because moisture darkens soil color.

107

Soils contain a variety of materials. Under the stereo microscope, natural materials (such as animal and plant matter) and artificial debris can be seen and identified. Often artificial debris can be found in a soil sample. This material can be helpful in determining the soil's origin. Artificial debris can include pieces of glass, paint chips, asphalt, brick fragments, and other items. These objects can make soil unique.

Under a compound light microscope, types of rocks and minerals can be identified. More than 2,200 types of minerals exist. Rocks are made of combinations of minerals, and exist in thousands of varieties.

Materials:

Soil sample from crime scene (Sample CS)
Soil sample from Terry's boots (Sample A)
Soil sample from Matt's boots (Sample B)
Soil sample from Spencer's boots (Sample C)
Soil sample from victim's yard (Sample D)
Soil sample from Terry's yard (Sample E)
Stereo microscope
Slides
Spoons or spatulas
Dissecting needles
Small metric ruler

Answers to Conclusion Questions of Investigation 2–6:

1. Soil at a crime scene can be transferred to other locations. It can be carried on a person's clothing or on a car. Soil that can be linked to a crime scene and a suspect can provide a link between the two.

2. pieces of glass, paint chips, asphalt, brick fragments, and other items

3. CS and A

4. CS and A

5. CS and A

6. CS and A

7. Yes, it is the same as sample A.

8. Answers will vary.

NSTA Objectives that apply to this investigation

As a result of activities in grades K–4, all students should develop:

■ abilities necessary to do scientific inquiry and understanding about scientific inquiry. Students should employ simple equipment and tools to gather data and extend the senses. Students should use data to construct a reasonable explanation. (*Elementary Standard, Science as Inquiry*)

■ an understanding of properties of earth materials, objects in the sky, and changes in earth and sky. Students should understand fundamental concepts and principles that underlie the properties of earth materials. Earth's materials have different physical and chemical properties. (*Elementary Standard, Earth and Space Science*)

■ an understanding of properties of earth materials, objects in the sky, and changes in earth and sky. Students should understand fundamental concepts and principles that underlie the properties of earth materials. Students should understand soils have properties of color and texture, capacity to retain water, and ability to support the growth of many kinds of plants. (*Elementary Standard, Earth and Space Science*)

As a result of activities in grades 5–8, all students should develop:

■ abilities necessary to do scientific inquiry and understandings about scientific inquiry. Students should use appropriate tools and techniques to gather, analyze, and interpret data. Students should think critically and logically to make the relationships between evidence and explanations. (*Grades 5–8 Standard, Science as Inquiry*)

■ understanding of structure of the earth system, Earth's history, and Earth in the solar system. Students should understand fundamental concepts and principles that underlie the understanding of the structure of the Earth system. Soil consists of weathered rocks and decomposed organic material from dead plants, animals, and bacteria. Soils are often found in layers, with each having a different chemical composition and texture. (*Grades 5–8 Standard, Earth Science*)

Name _____ Date _____

DIGGING UP CLUES
Student Investigator Page

The Crime

Matt McGhee owns and operates a landscaping company. Matt and his two employees, Terry and Spencer, specialize in removing unwanted trees from land where homes are being built. All three men wear heavy-duty, waterproof boots when they work.

When Matt and his crew arrived at the work site this morning, they found an abandoned car. Spencer called the police, and an investigator was sent over immediately. The car was quickly identified as one that had been stolen the night before. The car happened to have been stolen from Terry's neighbor.

The investigator carefully looked over the car, trying to find any clues about what had happened to it and how it had arrived on the work site. The investigator noticed that some of the dirt on the tires and wheels was recent. Most of the soil that he could see looked like dirt from the work site. However, this recent dirt was layered on top of some other soil. The bottom layer of dirt was clearly different from the work-site soil.

The investigator collected some of both layers of soil from the crime scene car. He carefully packed the soil samples in plastic bags and labeled them "Crime Scene Soil Samples—wheels of car." He then asked each member of Matt's team to give him some soil samples from their boots. He was suspicious of these men because one of them was a neighbor of the victim. Soil samples were also taken from the victim's yard, and from Terry's yard.

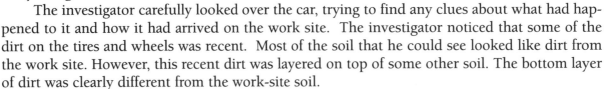

Soil can provide a link between the crime scene and the suspect.

Procedure

1. Place about one-half teaspoon of "Sample CS" on a microscope slide. Describe the color of the sample in the Data Table.

2. Place the slide under the stereo microscope and focus under low power. Then change to high power and sharpen the focus.

3. Examine the contents of the slide carefully. Separate the soil with the dissecting needle if necessary.

4. Count the number of pieces of plant matter in the sample. Record this number in the Data Table.

5. Count the number of soil particles that are larger than .5 millimeters (mm). Record this number in the Data Table.

6. Examine the soil for any artificial debris. List and describe the debris in the Data Table.

7. Repeat steps 1–6 for the other soil samples.

\multicolumn{5}{c}{**DATA TABLE. DESCRIPTION OF SOIL SAMPLES.**}
Samples	*Color*	*Number of pieces of plant matter*	*Particles larger than .5 mm*	*Type and number of artificial debris*
CS				
A				
B				
C				
D				
E				

Conclusion Questions

1. How can soil be used as evidence in a crime?

_____

_____

_____

2. What kinds of artificial debris might be found in soil?

_____

_____

_____

3. Which two soil samples are most alike in color?

_____

_____

_____

4. Which two soil samples are most alike in amount of plant matter they contain?

_____

_____

_____

5. Which two soil samples are most alike in number of particles larger than .5 mm?

_____

_____

_____

6. Which two soil samples are most alike in artificial debris?

_____

_____

_____

7. Based on your work, is the crime-scene soil sample the same as any of the other soil samples?

_____

_____

_____

8. Write an end to the crime story. Make sure your story corresponds to your findings in the lab.

_____

_____

_____

_____

_____

_____

_____

TEACHER INFORMATION

In this investigation, students must determine if a storeowner's claim—that his camping products are made from new materials with better insulation—is a crime of false advertisement. To solve whether the claim is true or false, they test seven different materials for insulating properties and heat retention.

Investigation Objectives:

Conduct tests that compare the amount of heat retained by hot water insulated with various materials.

Time Required: 40 minutes on Day 1
50 minutes on Day 2

Notes for the Teacher:

1. Read the Background to students, then have them read The Crime.

2. Arrange students in groups of 3 or 4. Give each group a copy of the Student Investigator Page.

3. A day or two prior to the lab, collect enough large self-locking bags so each group has seven bags. Each group will also need seven small jars and seven short thermometers. Each thermometer should fit inside a jar and each jar should fit inside a bag. Also collect pieces of fabric and other materials that can be used to line the inside of the bag. Some suggested materials include wool, flannel, feathers, thermal material, cotton, polyester, and rayon. If you cannot find some of these materials, you may substitute some other fabric or material. Place the material in separate piles in front of the room. For example, place the wool in the pile marked "Material A"; the cotton in the pile marked "Material B," etc. The fabric used to represent Kaleb's patented material (if you want Kaleb to be guilty of false advertisement) should be the same as one of the other fabrics used in piles A through F, but you may select a different color or texture.

4. The morning of Day 2 of the lab, boil several large containers of water and leave them heating until the temperature drops near 70° C. This water will be used by the students in the investigation activity. You will also need a large container of ice or access to a refrigerator. This will allow the students to expose the water to cold temperatures.

Background:

Certain materials retain heat better than others. When houses are built, materials are placed in the walls of the house to keep heat inside in the winter. These materials oppose the flow of energy through the walls to the outside. This type of material is called insulation.

Certain materials retain heat better than others. These materials are good insulators.

In the winter, we wear coats to keep us warm. Our body gives off heat that keeps us warm when it is cold outside. When we wear a coat, it keeps us from losing body heat. The material that makes up that coat will dictate how much heat we are able to retain on cold winter days.

Manufacturers of coats and sleeping bags have to consider the best material to use to make their coats. Some coats are lined with flannel, while others are stuffed with down. These materials help to insulate our bodies and prevent heat loss. Materials that prevent heat from leaving the body are good insulators. On cold winter days, you want to select a coat lined with material that provides good insulation.

Materials:

7 large self-locking plastic bags
7 thermometers
7 jars
Equal portions of insulating materials (you can vary the kinds, but some suggestions are flannel, wool, feathers, thermal, cotton, polyester, rayon)
Boiled water (about 70° C)
Refrigerator or cooler of ice
Clear tape

Answers to Conclusion Questions of Investigation 2–7

1. Answers will vary depending on materials used. Things like flannel and wool are good insulators.

2. Answers will vary depending on materials used. Materials like polyester and rayon are poor insulators.

3. Yes. Kaleb's material did not retain the heat in the water any longer than the other materials.

4. A large part of the human body is water.

5. Answers will vary.

NSTA objectives that apply to this investigation

As a result of activities in grades K–4, all students should develop:

- abilities necessary to do scientific inquiry and understanding about scientific inquiry. Students should employ simple equipment and tools to gather data and extend the senses. Students should use data to construct a reasonable explanation. (*Elementary Standard, Science as Inquiry*)

- an understanding of properties of earth materials, objects in the sky, and changes in earth and sky. Students should understand fundamental concepts and principles that underlie the properties of earth materials. Earth's materials have different physical and chemical properties. (*Elementary Standard, Earth and Space Science*)

As a result of activities in grades 5–8, all students should develop:

- understanding of structure of the earth system, Earth's history, and Earth in the solar system. Students should understand fundamental concepts and principles that underlie the understanding of science and technology in society. Technology influences society through its products and processes. Technology influences the quality of life and the ways people act and interact. (*Grades 5–8 Standard, Earth and Space Science*)

- understanding of structure of the earth system, Earth's history, and Earth in the solar system. Students should understand fundamental concepts and principles that underlie the understanding of science and technology in society. Scientists and engineers work in many different settings, including colleges and universities, businesses and industries, specific research institutes, and government agencies. (*Grades 5–8 Standard, Earth and Space Science*)

- understanding of science as a human endeavor, nature of science, and history of science. Students should understand fundamental concepts and principles that underlie the understanding of science as a human endeavor. Some scientists work in teams and some work alone, but all communicate extensively with others. (*Grades 5–8 Standard, History and Nature of Science*)

- understanding of science as a human endeavor, nature of science, and history of science. Students should understand fundamental concepts and principles that underlie the understanding of science as a human endeavor. Science requires different abilities, depending on such factors as the field of study and type of inquiry. The work of science relies on basic human qualities, such as reasoning, insight, energy, skill, and creativity—as well as on scientific habits of mind, such as intellectual honesty, tolerance of ambiguity, skepticism, and openness to new ideas. (*Grades 5–8 Standard, History and Nature of Science*)

Name _____   Date _____

The Truth Is in the Proof
Student Investigator Page

The Crime

Business is booming at Kaleb's Camping Supply Store. All day Monday, customers flocked in the store buying winter coats. All of this activity came after Kaleb placed the following advertisement in the local paper.

Kaleb's Camping Supply

Get the finest in camping wear! Our camping bags and winter coats are made of special patented material guaranteed to keep you warm in the coldest weather. This special material that lines our coats and camping bags can only be found at Kaleb's. We hold exclusive rights to this material.

No other coats compare, they wouldn't even dare! When you buy from Jackson's or Pete's, their low-quality outerwear can't compete.

Stay warmer in our better-quality coats and sleeping bags and enjoy our even lower price tags!

Kaleb Rameriz,
Owner

Elaine Jackson and Peter Rowe, owners of the other two camping supply stores in town, call the police department to register a complaint concerning Rameriz's advertisement. According to Elaine and Peter, there are no new patented insulating materials on the market. They believe Kaleb is guilty of false advertisement.

Police investigators—along with representatives from the Better Business Bureau—visit Kaleb Friday morning at his store. When questioned, Kaleb insists he had a special team of scientists develop this material to be placed in coats he sells. Kaleb refuses to provide the name of the special material or any further information.

> Certain materials retain heat better than others. These materials are good insulators.

After meeting with Peter and Elaine, police investigators decide the quickest way to solve this problem is with a little test. Samples of insulating material will be taken from the warmest jackets that Peter and Elaine sell and from the special patented jacket Kaleb sells. A test will be performed by lab scientists to determine which material retains the most heat. If Kaleb's special material proves to be the most effective insulating material, Kaleb's advertisement may be legitimate. If Kaleb's material proves no better than his competitors during testing, Kaleb has made a false advertisement, and a crime has been committed.

Procedure

Day 1: Preparing the insulated pouches

1. Label the seven plastic bags as A, B, C, D, E, F, and Kaleb. Material A through F is composed of material taken from Peter's and Elaine's coats. Kaleb's coat material will be used in the last bag.

2. Using clear tape, line plastic bag A with Material A. Only use one layer thick in your lining (Figure 15).

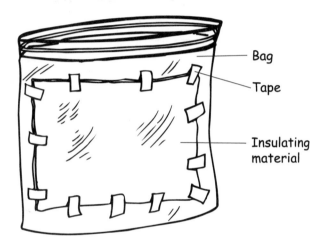

Figure 15. Lining the bag with insulating material.

3. Repeat step 2 lining bags B through F with materials B through F.

4. Repeat step 2 lining the bag marked "Kaleb" with the material designated as the patented material in Kaleb's coats.

5. Place the bags aside in preparation for tomorrow's experiment.

Day 2. Performing the experiment

6. Fill all seven jars with the boiled water prepared by your teacher; the water should have cooled to around 70° C. (CAUTION: Use the water only under teacher supervision.) Record the temperature of the water in the Data Table under "Starting temperature." These seven jars of water will represent the human body, since the human body is made of a large quantity of water.

7. Quickly drop a thermometer into each jar of water and seal the jar with a lid.

8. Place each jar in a lined plastic bag and lock the bag The plastic bags represent the insulated coats that cover the human body and keep it from losing heat.

9. Place each bag in a cold environment (either a refrigerator or cooler of ice).

10. Each 10 minutes for the next 40 minutes, quickly open each bag and observe the temperature of the jar inside. Record these temperatures in the proper location on the Data Table. Reseal the jar and close the bag as quickly as possible and return them to the cold environment until the next time to check the temperature.

		DATA TABLE. TEMPERATURES OF WATER IN EACH CONTAINER.			
Container	**Starting temperature**	**Temperature after 10 minutes**	**Temperature after 20 minutes**	**Temperature after 30 minutes**	**Temperature after 40 minutes**
A					
B					
C					
D					
E					
F					
Kaleb					

Conclusion Questions

1. Which bag had the best insulator in it?

   _____

   _____

   _____

2. Which bag had the poorest insulator in it?

   _____

   _____

   _____

3. According to the results of the activity, do you have proof that Kaleb made a false advertisement? Support your answer.

   _____

   _____

   _____

   _____

4. Why was water placed in the jars that represented the human body?

_____

_____

_____

_____

5. Write a two-paragraph conclusion as the ending of this story.

_____

_____

_____

_____

_____

_____

SECTION 3

LIFE SCIENCE

INVESTIGATION 3–1

A HAIRY SITUATION

TEACHER INFORMATION

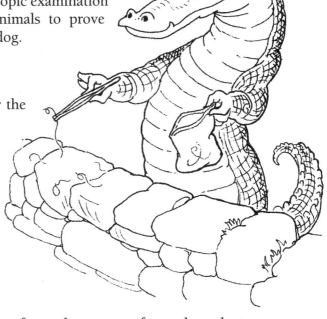

Challenge your students to solve this crime of dog-napping! They can do this by conducting microscopic examination of hair samples from humans and animals to prove whether Ron stole Doc, his neighbor's dog.

Investigation Objectives:

Observe human and animal hair under the microscope.
Determine if a strand of hair is human or animal.

Time Required: 50 minutes

Notes for the Teacher:

1. Read the Background to students, then have them read The Crime.

2. Copy the Student Investigator Page for each group or for each student.
Also photocopy figures 16 through 19 from the Background for your students or sketch these on the board prior to reading the Background to them. This activity is best done in groups of 2 or 3 students each.

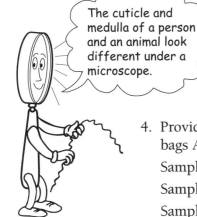

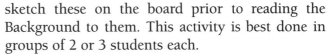
The cuticle and medulla of a person and an animal look different under a microscope.

3. Before the investigation, obtain some human head hair and some hair from a cat. Review with your students how to use a microscope. Show students how to make a wet mount of an object. Describe how to apply the cover slip at an angle.

4. Provide hair samples for your students in three bags. Label the bags A, B, and C.

   Sample A—human head hair

   Sample B—cat hair

   Sample C—human head hair

Background:

Hair is part of your skin. It grows out of an organ called the hair follicle. The length of a hair extends from the root within the follicle, up the shaft, to the tip (Figure 16). The shaft of the hair is made of three parts: cuticle, medulla, and cortex.

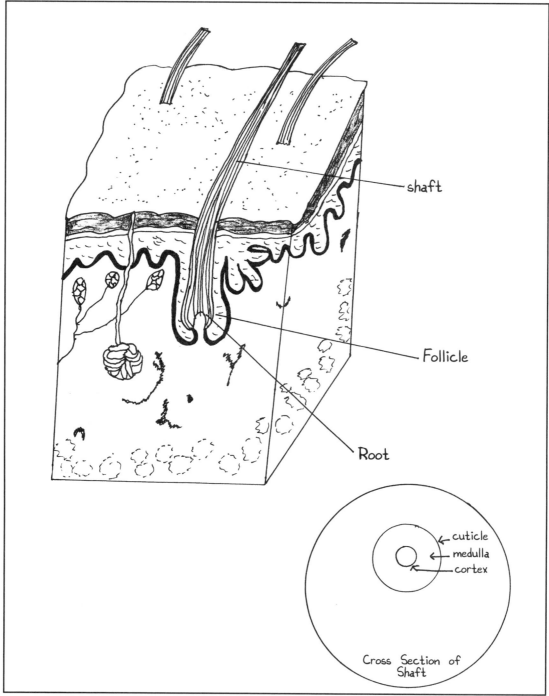

Figure 16. A human hair magnified.

The cuticle of a hair is very strong. It is made of overlapping scales that look like shingles on a roof. The cuticles of human and animal hairs have different patterns of scales.

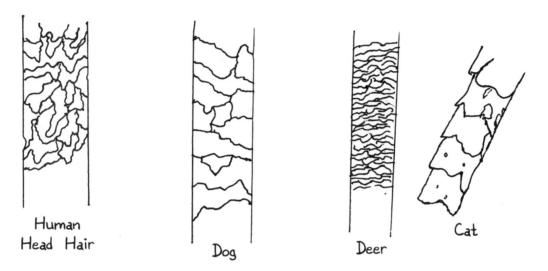

Figure 17. The scale patterns of humans and some animals.

The part of the hair inside the cuticle is the cortex. The cortex is actually a middle layer of the hair, between the cuticle and the inner medulla. Pigments in the cortex give the hair its color.

The medulla is the innermost layer, and it is made of a collection of cells. If you see these cells under the microscope, they seem to form a canal. The pattern and diameter of the medulla in human and in animal hairs is different. Therefore, the medulla can be used to distinguish between an animal and a human hair sample.

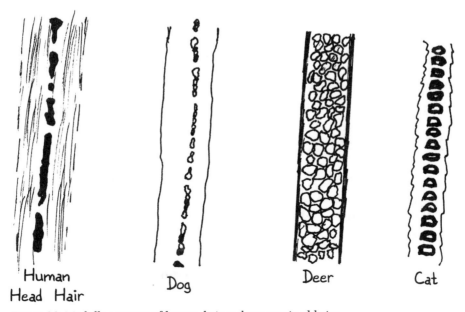

Figure 18. Medulla patterns of human hair and some animal hairs.

Sometimes medulla patterns are described according to how they are connected. The medulla can be a continuous line of cells, an interrupted pattern, or a fragmented pattern. Hair from human heads usually has a fragmented or missing medulla. The medulla of animal hair is generally continuous or interrupted.

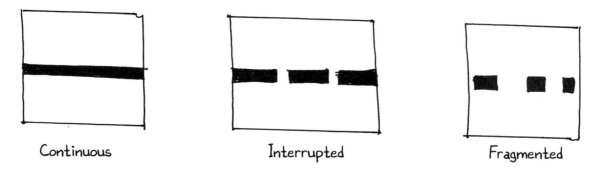

Continuous   Interrupted   Fragmented

Figure 19. Three basic types of medulla patterns.

Materials:

Compound microscope
Glass slide
Water
Forceps or tweezers
Hair samples
Medicine dropper

Answers to Conclusion Questions of Investigation 3–1:

1. Yes; cat

2. Yes; by the size and shape of the hairs' medulla

3. No; there was no dog hair on his clothes

4. Answers may vary; but no, there are other ways that Ron could have gotten dog hair on his clothes

5. Use Figure 16.

6. Answers will vary.

NSTA Objectives that apply to this investigation

As a result of activities in grades K–4, all students should develop:

- abilities necessary to do scientific inquiry and understanding about scientific inquiry. Students should employ simple equipment and tools to gather data and extend the senses. Students should use data to construct a reasonable explanation. (*Elementary Standard, Science as Inquiry*)

- abilities of technological design, understanding about science and technology, and abilities to distinguish between natural objects and objects made by humans. Students should understand fundamental concepts and principles that underlie the understanding about science and technology. Tools help scientists make better observations, measurements, and equipment for investigations. They help scientists see, measure, and do things that they could not otherwise see, measure, and do. (*Elementary Standard, Science and Technology*)

As a result of activities in grades 5–8, all students should develop:

- abilities necessary to do scientific inquiry and understandings about scientific inquiry. Students should use appropriate tools and techniques to gather, analyze, and interpret data. Students should think critically and logically to make the relationships between evidence and explanations. (*Grades 5–8 Standard, Science as Inquiry*)

- understanding of structure and function in living things, reproduction and heredity, regulation and behavior, populations and ecosystems, and diversity and adaptations of organisms. Students should understand fundamental concepts and principles that underlie the understanding of diversity and adaptations of organisms. Biological evolution accounts for the diversity of species developed through gradual processes over many generations. Species acquire many of their unique characteristics through biological adaptation, which involves the selection of naturally occurring variations in populations. Biological adaptations include changes in structures, behaviors, or physiology that enhance survival and reproductive success in a particular environment. (*Grades 5–8 Standard, Life Science*)

- abilities necessary to do scientific inquiry and understandings about scientific inquiry. Students should understand fundamental concepts and principles that underlie the understanding about the abilities necessary to do scientific inquiry. Students should think critically and logically to make the relationships between evidence and explanations. Students should be able to review data from a simple experiment, summarize the data, and form a logical argument about the cause-and-effect relationships in the experiment. (*Grades 5–8 Standard, Science as Inquiry*)

Name _____ Date _____

A HAIRY SITUATION
Student Investigator Page

The Crime

Ron Mann is in trouble. He was stopped by the police this morning on the way to work. They took him to the police station because he is a suspect in a dog-napping.

Ron's next-door neighbor, Connie, called the police. Connie claims that early this morning, she saw a man grab her dog, Doc, and run behind Ron's house. She thinks the man she saw was Ron. Ron often complains about Doc's late-night barking and has threatened to call the dog pound. She also said that the man who picked up Doc was wearing a dark suit and tie and had red hair like Ron's.

When picked up for questioning, Ron was wearing a dark suit and tie. However, Ron denied touching Doc. Police pointed out that if Ron did steal Doc, there would be dog hairs on his clothing. Ron agreed to let police take hair samples from his suit and test them. He was confident there would be no dog hair on his suit because he had no dogs at home and was allergic to dog hair. Ron did tell police he owned a cat named Stingray. Investigators assured Ron that cat and dog hair appeared very different microscopically. Ron felt confident this hair test would clear him of any wrongdoing.

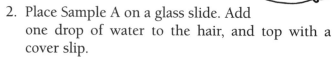

Procedure

1. Obtain hair sample A taken from Ron's clothing.

2. Place Sample A on a glass slide. Add one drop of water to the hair, and top with a cover slip.

3. Use the microscope to observe the medulla of the hair. Draw the hair and medulla in the Data Table under Sample A.

4. Repeat the same process using both Sample B and Sample C. Draw each hair and medulla in the Data Table under samples B and C.

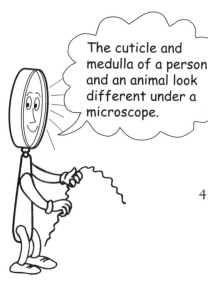

The cuticle and medulla of a person and an animal look different under a microscope.

DATA TABLE. DRAWINGS OF HAIRS AND MEDULLAS.		
Sample A	*Sample B*	*Sample C*

Conclusion Questions

1. Did Ron have any animal hair on his clothing? If so, what type of animal hair?

   _____

   _____

2. Did Ron have human hair on his clothes? How do you know?

   _____

   _____

3. Based on your results, did Ron steal Doc? Explain your answer.

   _____

   _____

   _____

4. Would the presence of dog hair on Ron have proven that he definitely stole Doc? Explain your answer.

   _____

   _____

   _____

5. Draw and describe the three parts of a hair shaft.

6. Finish this story by writing a one-paragraph ending. Describe what happened to Doc in light of the results of your investigation. Be creative.

   _____

   _____

   _____

   _____

   _____

   _____

   _____

INVESTIGATION 3–2

LEARNING FROM LIPSTICK

TEACHER INFORMATION

When a napkin with red lipstick is found at the spot where the basketball uniform money was stolen, all the women in the gym wearing red lipstick are asked to make a lip print on a napkin. Students compare lip patterns with a magnifying glass to identify the culprit.

Investigation Objective:

Compare the lip prints of the five suspects to evidence at the crime scene.

Time Required: 50 minutes

Notes for the Teacher:

1. Read the Background to students, then have them read The Crime. Photocopy Figure 20 from the Background for your students to use as you read the material to them.

2. Copy the Student Investigator Page for each student or for each group of students. This activity is best done in groups of 2 or 3 students.

3. Obtain several tubes of red lipstick and some white paper towels.

4. A few days before the investigation, ask 5 females to make lip prints. Have one female make about 10 lip prints on separate pieces of white paper towel. At the bottom of 5 of the paper towels, write the name of the person making the print. On the other 5 paper towels, write the words "Crime Scene Print." Ask the other four females to make 5 paper towel prints. Write the name of the lip print owner on each of these 5 paper towels.

5. The day of the investigation, give each group of students one crime scene print and a name-labeled print from each of the 5 females (now called suspects). If there are more student groups than prints, prints can be shared. Each group will have one paper towel labeled crime scene and five paper towels with a different person's name on each.

Most people's lip prints show parts of at least two print patterns.

Background:

Have you ever picked up a glass and seen a lipstick print on it? Women wearing lipstick leave visible prints on everything from glassware to tissues. Even though you have heard a lot about fingerprints, you have probably seen many more lip prints than fingerprints.

You may not realize it but the skin on your lips creates patterns. Most people's lips show parts of at least two patterns. Vertical grooves, rectangular grooves, branching grooves, and diamond grooves are four common lip patterns (Figure 20).

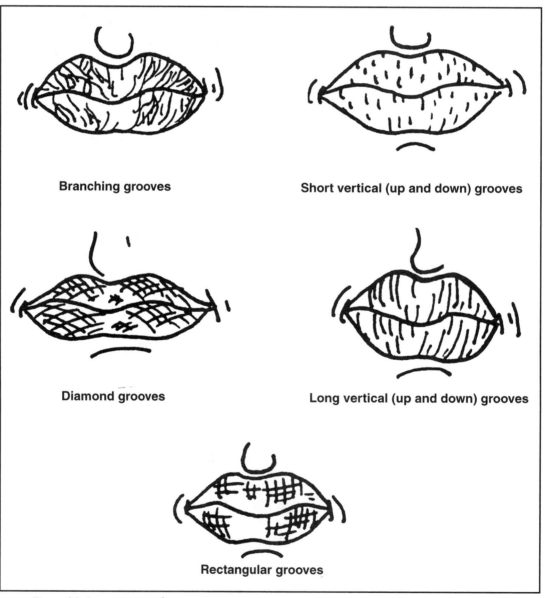

Figure 20. Some common lip patterns.

The lip patterns left at a crime scene can be matched to the lip patterns of a suspect. Lipstick prints on drinking glasses and on tissues can be important clues in solving crimes.

Materials:

Suspect lipstick prints
Crime scene lipstick print
Paper towels
Magnifying glass

Answers to Conclusion Questions of Investigation 3–2:

1. Yes. One print taken from a suspect matches the crime scene print.

2. Answers will vary depending on the prints used.

3. Yes. Different people have different lip patterns.

4. Nose prints are unique to horses and can be used to identify a particular horse.

NSTA Objectives that apply to this investigation

As a result of activities in grades K–4, all students should develop:

- abilities necessary to do scientific inquiry and understanding about scientific inquiry. Students should use data to construct a reasonable explanation. (*Elementary Standard, Science as Inquiry*)

- an understanding of characteristics of organisms, life cycle of organisms, and organisms and the environment. Students should recognize that each plant or animal has different structures that serve different functions in growth, survival, and reproduction. (*Elementary Standard, Life Science*)

As a result of activities in grades 5–8, all students should develop:

- abilities necessary to do scientific inquiry and understandings about scientific inquiry. Students should understand fundamental concepts and principles that underlie the understanding about the abilities necessary to do scientific inquiry. Students should think critically and logically to make the relationships between evidence and explanations. Students should be able to review data from a simple experiment, summarize the data, and form a logical argument about the cause-and-effect relationships in the experiment. (*Grades 5–8 Standard, Science as Inquiry*)

- understanding of structure and function in living things, reproduction and heredity, regulation and behavior, populations and ecosystems, and diversity and adaptations of organisms. Students should understand fundamental concepts and principles that underlie the understanding of diversity and adaptations of organisms. Biological evolution accounts for the diversity of species developed through gradual processes over many generations. Species acquire many of their unique characteristics through biological adaptation, which involves the selection of naturally occurring variations in populations. Biological adaptations include changes in structures, behaviors, or physiology that enhance survival and reproductive success in a particular environment. (*Grades 5–8 Standard, Life Science*)

■ abilities necessary to do scientific inquiry and understandings about scientific inquiry. Students should understand fundamental concepts and principles that underlie the understanding about the abilities necessary to do scientific inquiry. Students should develop descriptions, explanations, predictions, and models using evidence. (*Grades 5–8, Science as Inquiry*)

Name _____ Date _____

LEARNING FROM LIPSTICK
Student Investigator Page

The Crime

Last night was the opening of basketball season for the Central Middle School Hornets. To raise money to buy new boys' and girls' uniforms, parents set up a concession stand at the game. The gym was packed with spectators and concession sales were excellent. More than enough money was raised for the uniforms.

After the game, the crowd filed out of the auditorium. With about 30 people still left in the gym, the lights suddenly went out. In the darkness, someone ran to the person counting the money and snatched a handful of bills. The person counting the bills shouted for security to lock the exits. When the lights were turned on, a napkin with red lip marks on it was found on the floor where the money was being counted.

Most people's lip prints show parts of at least two print patterns.

An announcement was made for everyone to sit in the bleachers. The security guard scanned the crowd for women wearing red lipstick. He asked each of these women if they would help him find the thief. The women agreed. They applied their lipstick and made a lip print on a napkin. Your job is to decide if one of these women was the thief by comparing the print on the dropped napkin with the prints collected by the security guard.

Procedure

1. Obtain a sample of the crime scene print found on the dropped napkin.

2. Use a magnifying glass to examine the print.

3. In the Data Table, draw a picture of the lip pattern revealed in this print.

4. Obtain the lip prints from the five suspects.

5. Use a magnifying glass and examine each lip print of the five suspects.

6. Place the name of each suspect in the Data Table.

7. Draw the lip pattern of each suspect's lip print in the Data Table.

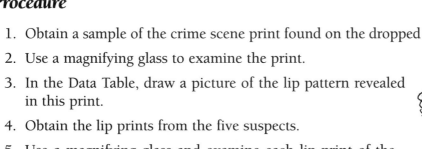

DATA TABLE. SKETCHES OF LIP PRINTS EXAMINED.

Crime Scene Lip Print

Suspect # 1 _____

Suspect # 2 _____

Suspect # 3 _____

Suspect # 4 _____

Suspect # 5 _____

Conclusion Questions

1. Did one of the suspects commit the crime? Explain your answer.

   _____

   _____

   _____

   _____

   _____

   _____

2. In your own words, describe what the patterns on each of the lip prints look like to you. For example, you might say that Suspect 1 had long vertical grooves, Suspect B had diamond grooves, Crime Scene Print had branching grooves, etc.

   Crime Scene Print: _____

   _____

   Suspect 1: _____

   _____

   Suspect 2: _____

   _____

   Suspect 3: _____

   _____

   Suspect 4: _____

   _____

   Suspect 5: _____

   _____

3. Do you think lip prints, like fingerprints, are unique to the person? Explain your answer.

   _____

   _____

   _____

   _____

4. Why do you think some horse owners record their horses' nose prints?

   _____

   _____

   _____

   _____

   _____

INVESTIGATION 3–3
"LEAFING" THE CRIME SCENE

TEACHER INFORMATION

Students investigate this robbery using leaf evidence. The robber backed his pickup truck into a tree before speeding away. Detectives searched the area for trucks matching the description, then collected and labeled leaves found in the trucks. Students compare leaf patterns and other characteristics to those from the tree at the scene to solve the crime.

Investigation Objective:

Compare characteristics of different leaves.

Time Required: 50 minutes

Notes for the Teacher:

1. Read the Background to students, then have them read The Crime.

2. Copy the Student Investigator Page for each student or for each group of students. Also copy Figure 21 for each group of students to use in this investigation. This activity is best done in groups of 2 or 3 students.

3. The day before the investigation, remove a small, leafy branch from nine different kinds of trees. Remove two branches from a 10th kind of tree you will select as the crime scene tree.

4. Place the branches in water so they will be fresh for the next day.

5. On the morning of the investigation, label 10 bags with the numbers 1 through 10 and one as "Ernest's yard." Remove all the leaves from the two branches of the tree you selected as the crime scene tree. Place some of these in the bag marked "Ernest's yard" and the rest of them in the bag marked "#4." Fill the remaining bags with leaves from the other types of trees.

Background:

Much of the work done in crime labs is comparative; that is, objects are often compared with one another. For example, a paint chip found on a hit-and-run victim's clothing may be compared with paint from a suspect's car. Establishing a match of these paint chips can help link the suspect to the crime.

Plant materials from a crime scene can even be compared with known plant parts. Botanists, scientists who study plants, can be called in to work on these cases. These scientists have no trouble identifying a tree from its parts, such as bark or leaves.

Leaves are the most obvious characteristic of trees. That is why many people learn to identify trees by their leaves. When examining a leaf, there are categories of features to consider: texture, margins, shape, and vein arrangement. These four categories are illustrated in Figure 21.

a. The texture of most leaves is smooth. However, some plants produce leaves with "hairy" areas. The so-called "hairy" parts are not made of hair, but of plant cells that extend out from the surface of the leaf.

b. The margin of a leaf is its outer edge. Three types of leaf margins are smooth, toothed, and lobed. Smooth margins have no indentations. Toothed margins look a little like the blade of a knife. Lobed margins have deep indentations. Some leaves have bristles, or pointed parts, on the tips of their lobes.

c. Leaves come in a variety of shapes. The base, the tip, and the overall leaf have a distinctive shape.

d. Nutrients and water are delivered to all parts of a leaf by its veins. If a leaf has one large vein through the middle, its venation is described as "pinnate." If more than one large vein extend from the base through the leaf, its venation is described as "palmate."

> Texture, shape, venation, and margin design of a leaf can be used to identify a tree by its leaves.

Materials:

Leaf from Ernest's tree
Leaf from each of the 10 suspects' trucks
11 pieces of white paper
Crayons

I. Texture:

II. Margins of leaves: (Edges-outside)

III. Shapes

1. Of tip

2. Of base

3. Overall

IV. Vein arrangement

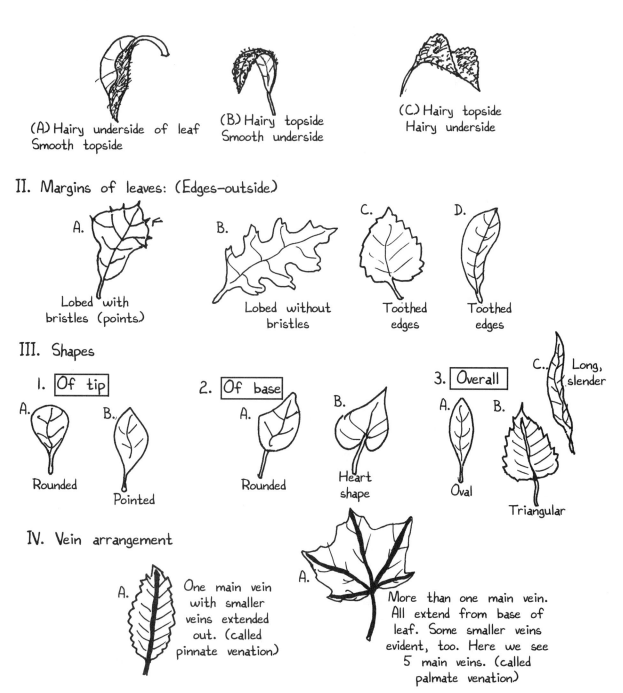

Figure 21. Four categories of leaf features.

Answers to Conclusion Questions of Investigation 3–3:

1. Yes, the leaves from Ernest's tree matched the leaves from truck 4.

2. to preserve the appearance of the leaf after the leaf is dead and dry

3. Answer will depend on the leaf selected by teacher.

4. Answer will depend on the leaves selected by teacher.

5. Botanists study plants.

NSTA Objectives that apply to this investigation

As a result of activities in grades K–4, all students should develop:

- abilities necessary to do scientific inquiry and understanding about scientific inquiry. Students should use data to construct a reasonable explanation. (*Elementary Standard, Science as Inquiry*)

As a result of activities in grades 5–8, all students should develop:

- abilities necessary to do scientific inquiry and understanding about scientific inquiry. Students should use appropriate tools and techniques to gather, analyze, and interpret data. Students should think critically and logically to make the relationships between evidence and explanations. (*Grades 5–8 Standard, Science as Inquiry*)

- an understanding that biological evolution accounts for the diversity of species developed through gradual processes over many generations and species acquire many of their unique characteristics through biological adaptation. (*Grades 5–8 Standard, Science as Inquiry*)

- understanding of structure and function in living things, reproduction and heredity, regulation and behavior, populations and ecosystems, and diversity and adaptations of organisms. Students should understand fundamental concepts and principles that underlie the understanding of diversity and adaptations of organisms. Biological evolution accounts for the diversity of species developed through gradual processes over many generations. Species acquire many of their unique characteristics through biological adaptation, which involves the selection of naturally occurring variations in populations. Biological adaptations include changes in structures, behaviors, or physiology that enhance survival and reproductive success in a particular environment. (*Grades 5–8 Standard, Life Science*)

- abilities necessary to do scientific inquiry and understanding about scientific inquiry. Students should understand fundamental concepts and principles that underlie the understanding about the abilities necessary to do scientific inquiry. Students should think critically and logically to make the relationships between evidence and explanations. Students should be able to review data from a simple experiment, summarize the data, and form a logical argument about the cause-and-effect relationships in the experiment. (*Grades 5–8 Standard, Science as Inquiry*)

Name _____ **Date** _____

"LEAFING" THE CRIME SCENE
Student Investigator Page

The Crime

Ernest and Joy Mason were robbed last night. Ernest witnessed some important events before the robber escaped. He gave the following statement to police.

"I was sleeping soundly when I heard a sound of a truck outside. The clock said 3:22 A.M. I threw on my robe and ran to the front door. As I opened it, I saw a green, extended-cab pickup truck back into a tree near our driveway. I couldn't see the license plate as it sped away, but I could see that it was a local plate. Leaves and limbs were knocked from the tree. I'm sure some of these fell into the back of the truck. I don't think the impact made any dents on the truck because of the rubber bumper."

Detectives noted that the tree the truck hit is fairly unusual for this area of the country. They felt that the tree could be a valuable clue for solving this crime.

Detectives obtained the names of all local owners of green, extended-cab trucks. Officers visited each owner and looked in the backs of their trucks for evidence. Each time leaves or limbs were found, detectives bagged and labeled them. At the end of their search, they had found ten trucks with leaves in them.

The investigators of this crime need some help identifying these leaves. You can help decide if the leaves on Ernest's damaged tree match leaves found in the back of any of the ten trucks.

Procedure

1. Obtain 11 pieces of unlined white paper. At the bottom of one paper write "Leaf from Ernest's yard." On the bottom of another paper write "Truck 1." On the bottom of

a third piece of paper write "Truck 2." Continue this process until you have labeled all 11 pieces of paper.

> Texture, shape, venation, and margin design of a leaf can be used to identify a tree by its leaves.

2. Obtain a sample of each of the 11 leaves. Place each leaf on top of the appropriate piece of paper. Also get a copy of Figure 21 from your teacher.

3. On the Data Table, make the following observations about all 11 leaves. Use Figure 21 to help you classify the types.

   a. Under the column marked "Texture," note if the leaves are hairy on the top side, underside, both sides, or neither side.

   b. Under the column called "Margin," classify the leaves as lobed with bristles, lobed without bristles, toothed edges, smooth edges, or none of these.

   c. Under "Shape of Tip," indicate if the tips are round or pointed.

   d. For "Shape of Base," note if they are round, heart-shaped, or neither.

   e. Note under "Overall Shape" if the leaves are more oval, triangular, or slender. If they are none of those, indicate "none of these."

   f. Under "Vein Arrangement," write if the veins are pinnate (one main vein with small ones extending from it) or palmate (all main veins extend from base of leaf).

4. To preserve evidence for the trial long after the leaf dries and gets brittle, make a leaf rubbing of each leaf on the appropriate piece of paper. To make a leaf rubbing:

   a. Place the leaf, top side up, on a desk.

   b. Cover the leaf with a sheet of white paper.

   c. Peel the paper from a crayon, then lay the crayon on its side on the paper. Rub the crayon sideways back and forth across the paper. Rub the entire section of the leaf under the paper until the leaf is exposed in the rubbing.

   d. Label the location where a leaf was found on its leaf rubbing.

5. Staple your leaf rubbings to your lab report when you turn it in to your teacher.

DATA TABLE. DESCRIPTION OF LEAVES FROM TRUCKS AND FROM ERNEST'S TREE.						
Leaf	*Texture*	*Margin*	*Shape of tip*	*Shape of base*	*Overall shape*	*Vein arrangement*
Leaf from tree in Ernest's yard						
Truck 1						
Truck 2						
Truck 3						
Truck 4						
Truck 5						
Truck 6						
Truck 7						
Truck 8						
Truck 9						
Truck 10						

Conclusion Questions

1. Did one of the leaves from the truck match the leaves from the tree in Ernest's yard? Which one?

   _____

   _____

   _____

2. What was the purpose of making a leaf rubbing?

   _____

   _____

   _____

3. Was the leaf from the crime scene a palmate or pinnate leaf?

   _____

   _____

   _____

4. Were most of the leaves you examined today palmate or pinnate?

   _____

   _____

   _____

5. What does a botanist study?

   _____

   _____

   _____

INVESTIGATION 3–4

A SPOOKY CROOK

TEACHER INFORMATION

This investigation involves the Halloween prank of a robbery of skeleton bones from 20 different middle school labs. The bones have been recovered, but they're all mixed up! The students' job is to reassemble the right-sized bones onto a partial skeleton.

Investigation Objectives:

Assemble a human skeleton correctly.

Time Required: 50 minutes

Notes for the Teacher:

1. Read the Background to students, then have them read The Crime.

2. Copy a Student Investigator Page for each student or for each group of students. This activity is best done in groups of 2 or 3 students. Photocopy Worksheets 1 and 2 and Figure 22 from the Background for each group of students.

Background:

Most people have 206 bones in their skeleton.

At some point in your science studies you will study the human skeleton. Your skeleton has several important functions. It supports the body and protects its internal organs. It works with your muscles to help your body to move. Some bones of the skeleton make blood cells and release important minerals.

The central portion of a human skeleton is made of the skull, vertebral column, and rib cage. The remaining bones are attached to this central portion. Most people have a total of 206 individual bones in their skeleton (Figure 22).

Human anatomy is the study of the structure of your body. Knowledge of anatomy can be helpful to people studying crimes. Knowing the parts of the human body is also important in any type of medical career.

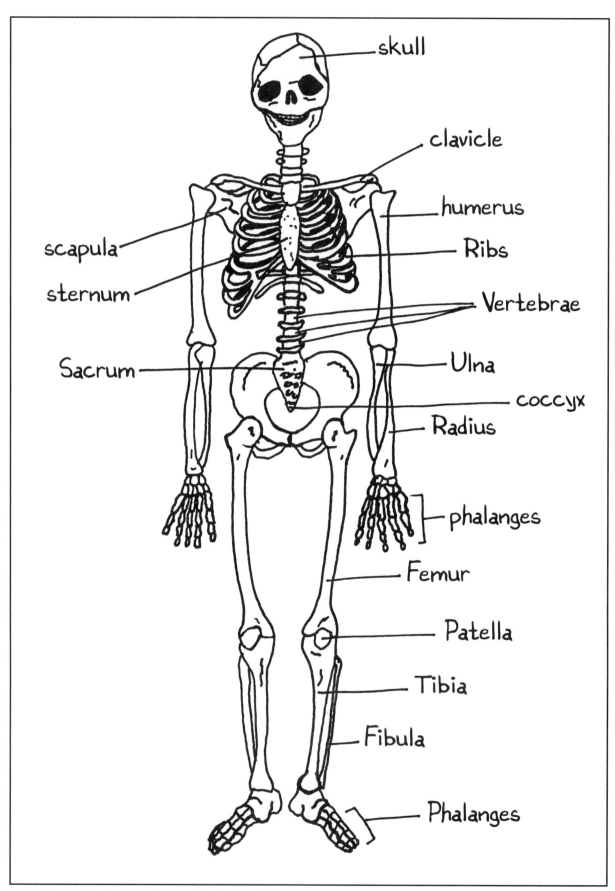

Figure 22. The major bones of the human skeleton.

Materials:

Scissors
Tape
Worksheets 1 and 2

Answers to Conclusion Questions of Investigation 3–4:

1. X, R, K, I, C, J, Q, D, S, O, F, B, P, G, AA, N, M, T, V

2. A, BB, E, Y, Z, H, L, U

3. a. femur; b. humerus; c. scapula; d. ulna, radius; e. tibia, fibula; f. patella; g. sacrum

4. The study of the structure of the body.

5. Answers will vary.

NSTA Objectives that apply to this investigation

As a result of activities in grades K–4, all students should develop:

■ abilities necessary to do scientific inquiry and understanding about scientific inquiry. Students should use data to construct a reasonable explanation. (*Elementary Standard, Science as Inquiry*)

As a result of activities in grades 5–8, all students should develop:

■ abilities necessary to do scientific inquiry and understandings about scientific inquiry. Students should use appropriate tools and techniques to gather, analyze, and interpret data. Students should think critically and logically to make the relationships between evidence and explanations. (*Grades 5–8 Standard, Science as Inquiry*)

■ an understanding of structure and function in living things, reproduction and heredity, regulation and behavior, populations and ecosystems, and diversity and adaptations of organisms. Students should understand fundamental concepts and principles that underlie the understanding of structure and function in living systems. The human organism has systems for digestion, respiration, reproduction, circulation, excretion, movement, control, and coordination, and for protection from disease. These systems interact with one another. (*Grades 5–8 Standard, Life Science*)

■ abilities necessary to do scientific inquiry and understandings about scientific inquiry. Students should understand fundamental concepts and principles that underlie the understanding about the abilities necessary to do scientific inquiry. Students should develop descriptions, explanations, predictions, and models using evidence. (*Grades 5–8, Science as Inquiry*)

■ understanding of science as a human endeavor, nature of science, and history of science. Students should understand fundamental concepts and principles that underlie the understanding of science as a human endeavor. Some scientists work in teams and some work alone, but all communicate extensively with others. (*Grades 5–8 Standard, History and Nature of Science*)

- abilities necessary to do scientific inquiry and understanding about scientific inquiry. Students should understand fundamental concepts and principles that underlie the understanding about the abilities necessary to do scientific inquiry. Students should understand that different kinds of questions suggest different kinds of scientific investigations. Some investigations involve observing and describing objects, organisms, or events; some involve collecting specimens; some involve seeking more information; some involve discovery of new objects and phenomena; and some involve making models. (*Grades 5–8, Science as Inquiry*)

Name _____ Date _____

A Spooky Crook
Student Investigator Page

The Crime

Halloween was last week. During that week 20 local middle school science labs were robbed. Police feel the crimes were committed by holiday pranksters. In each robbery, bones were stolen from models of human skeletons in the lab.

Today police officers arrested a 21-year-old male. In his apartment they found a box of bones. It is believed that these bones belong to the skeletons in the middle school science labs. The box of bones is being carried to all 20 schools so that stolen bones can be correctly replaced on skeletons.

The bones arrived at your school today. You are on the team responsible for finding the correct bones to fit your skeleton. Any bones that don't belong to your skeleton should be placed back in the box to go to the next school.

Procedure

1. Use scissors to cut out each bone from Worksheet 1.

2. Worksheet 2 is a picture of the partial skeleton that was left after the robbery. Using Figure 22 as a reference, locate the bones that go on your partial skeleton.

3. Tape each bone in the correct location on Worksheet 2 until the skeleton is once again complete.

Most people have 206 bones in their skeleton.

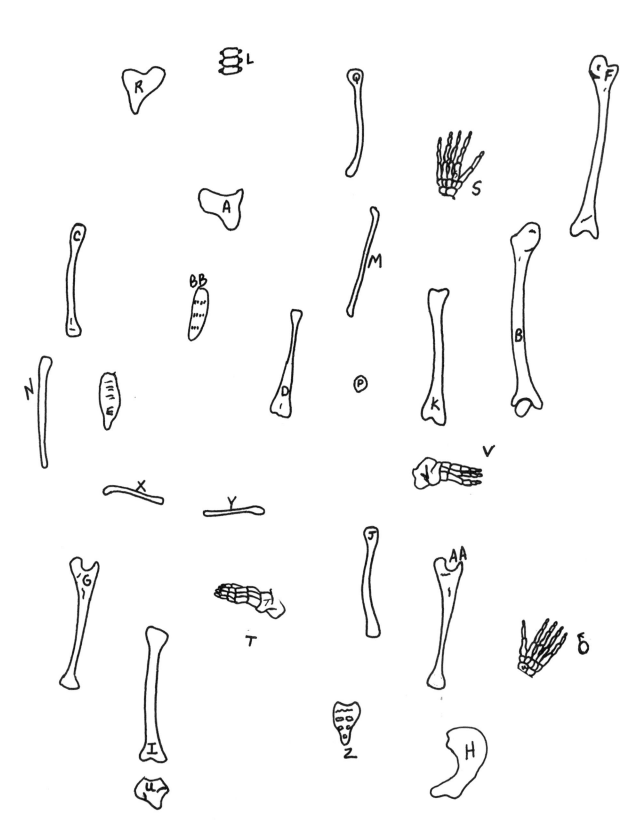

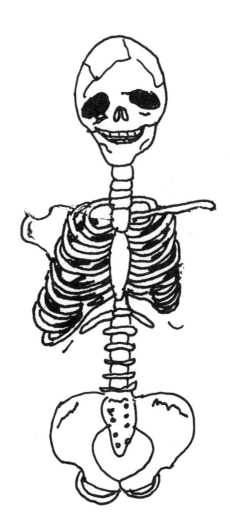

Conclusion Questions

1. List the letters of all the bones you placed on your partial skeleton on Worksheet 2.

   _____

   _____

2. List the letters of the bones you did not use that would be sent to another school.

   _____

   _____

3. Give the name of the following bones:

   a. upper leg or thigh: _____

   b. upper arm: _____

   c. shoulder: _____

   d. two bones of lower arm: _____

   e. two bones of lower leg: _____

   f. kneecap: _____

   g. bone directly above the coccyx: _____

4. Define anatomy.

   _____

   _____

   _____

5. Write a one-paragraph conclusion to this crime story. In this conclusion, describe how your team decided which bones to attach to the skeleton and which to place back in the box.

   _____

   _____

   _____

   _____

   _____

   _____

   _____

   _____

INVESTIGATION 3–5

PHARAOH'S FEMUR

TEACHER INFORMATION

A museum awaiting the shipment of an Egyptian Pharaoh's remains finds they were on an airplane with four other boxes of human remains. In the high humidity, labels slipped off the boxes. Since documents show the Pharaoh's height, students can measure the femurs in each box, using reproducible bone models, to solve the identity plight.

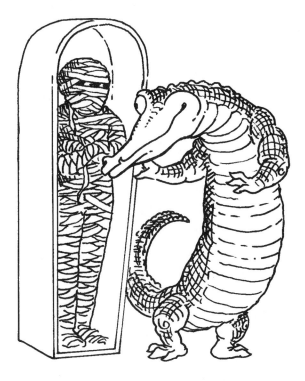

Investigation Objective:

Determine the height of a person using the length of his or her femur.

Time Required: 50 minutes

Notes for the Teacher:

1. Read the Background to students, then have them read The Crime.

2. Copy the Student Investigator Page for each student or for each group of students. This activity is best done in groups of 2 or 3 students. Photocopy the worksheets of femurs A, B, C, D, and E so each group or individual has one copy of the five different bones.

3. Show students where their femur is located on their bodies. Have students use a tape measure to try to determine the length of their own femurs.

Background:

Scientists have discovered a link between leg bone length and height of an individual. The thigh or upper leg contains a very large bone called the femur. The femur is located between the pelvis and the knee. (See Figure 23.) If you find the length of this bone in centimeters, you can use this length in a math equation to find the height of the owner of the femur. The math formula is:

$$2.6 \times \text{femur length (cm)} + 65 = \text{height in cm}$$

This height in centimeters can be converted to inches by multiplying your answer by 0.4. To give you some perspective on heights, a 6-foot individual is 72 inches or 183 cm tall (2.54 cm equals 1 inch).

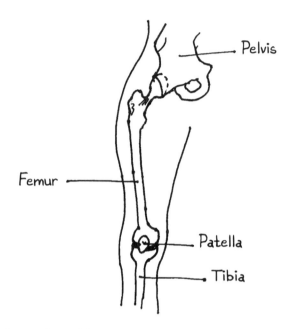

Figure 23. The femur is located between the pelvis and the knee. Its length can be inserted into a formula to determine the height of the owner of that bone.

Materials:

Scissors
Metric tape measure
Clear tape
Calculator (*optional*)
Worksheets A, B, C, D, and E

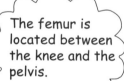

Answers to Data Table 1 of Investigation 3–5:

Femur	Length in cm
A	43.8
B	41.4
C	45.4
D	37.0
E	47.7

Answers to Conclusion Questions of Investigation 3–5:

1. Data Table 2.

DATA TABLE 2. HEIGHT OF OWNERS OF EACH FEMUR.		
Femur	*Demonstration of Work*	*Answer in cm*
A	43.8 × 2.6 + 65 =	178.88
B	41.4 × 2.6 + 65 =	172.64
C	45.4 × 2.6 + 65 =	183.04
D	37.0 × 2.6 + 65 =	161.20
E	47.7 × 2.6 + 65 =	189.02

2. C

3. D

4. It depends on the height of the students. The shortest person was 5 feet 4 inches tall. If anyone in the class is that tall, the answer is *yes*. If not, the answer is *no*.

5. Answers will vary.

NSTA Objectives that apply to this investigation

As a result of activities in grades K–4, all students should develop:

- abilities necessary to do scientific inquiry and understanding about scientific inquiry. Students should employ simple equipment and tools to gather data and extend the senses. Students should use data to construct a reasonable explanation. (*Elementary Standard, Science as Inquiry*)

- an understanding of characteristics of organisms, life cycle of organisms, and organisms and the environment. Students should recognize that each plant or animal has different structures that serve different functions in growth, survival, and reproduction. (*Elementary Standard, Life Science*)

- abilities of technological design, understanding about science and technology, and abilities to distinguish between natural objects and objects made by humans. Students should understand fundamental concepts and principles that underlie the understanding about science and technology. Tools help scientists make better observations, measurements, and equipment for investigations. They help scientists see, measure, and do things that they could not otherwise see, measure, and do. (*Elementary Standard, Science and Technology*)

As a result of activities in grades 5–8, all students should develop:

- understanding of structure and function in living things, reproduction and heredity, regulation and behavior, populations and ecosystems, and diversity and adaptations of organisms. Students should understand fundamental concepts and principles that underlie the understanding of structure and function in living systems. The human organism has systems for digestion, respiration, reproduction, circulation, excretion, movement, control, and coordination, and for protection from disease. These systems interact with one another. (*Grades 5–8 Standard, Life Science*)

- an understanding of structure and function in living things, reproduction and heredity, regulation and behavior, populations and ecosystems, and diversity and adaptations of organisms. Students should understand fundamental concepts and principles that underlie the understanding of diversity and adaptations of organisms. Biological evolution accounts for the diversity of species developed through gradual processes over many generations. Species acquire many of their unique characteristics through biological adaptation, which involves the selection of naturally occurring variations in populations. Biological adaptations include changes in structures, behaviors, or physiology that enhance survival and reproductive success in a particular environment. (*Grades 5–8 Standard, Life Science*)

- abilities necessary to do scientific inquiry and understanding about scientific inquiry. Students should understand fundamental concepts and principles that underlie the understanding about the abilities necessary to do scientific inquiry. Students should use mathematics in all aspects of scientific inquiry. Mathematics can be used to ask questions; to gather, organize, and present data; and to structure convincing explanations. (*Grades 5–8, Science as Inquiry*)

Name _____ Date _____

PHARAOH'S FEMUR
Student Investigator Page

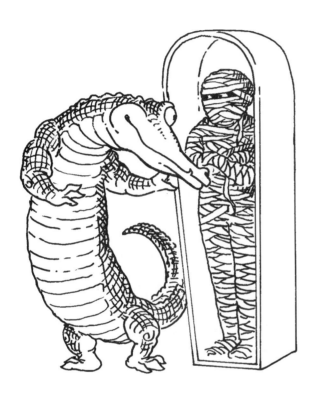

The Crime

The famous Roth Museum is eagerly awaiting a special shipment from Egypt: the remains of an ancient Egyptian Pharaoh. The Pharaoh's remains are worth more than one million dollars!

The shipment arrives by airplane at the expected time. Unfortunately, a terrible mistake happened. Four other boxes of human remains from Egypt are also aboard this airplane. Because of the high humidity in the cargo area, the names on the boxes have slipped off. No one knows which box contains the Pharaoh's remains.

After much thought, authorities decide to examine the femurs in each box to figure out which is the Pharaoh's. Documents at the museum show that the Pharaoh was 183 cm (or 72 inches) tall. Scientists measure the femurs in the five boxes to determine the heights of the individuals.

Procedure

1. Use scissors to cut out the two parts of the femur in Worksheet A.

2. Join the two pieces of the femur at the proper location. Tape this together and write "A" on the femur.

3. Repeat steps 1 and 2 using Worksheets B, C, D, and E. Label each femur with its appropriate letter.

4. On femur A, measure the distance between the two most distant points.

5. Record the length of femur A on Data Table 1 in the proper column.

6. Repeat steps 4 and 5 for femurs B, C, D, and E. Record their lengths in the proper location on Data Table 1.

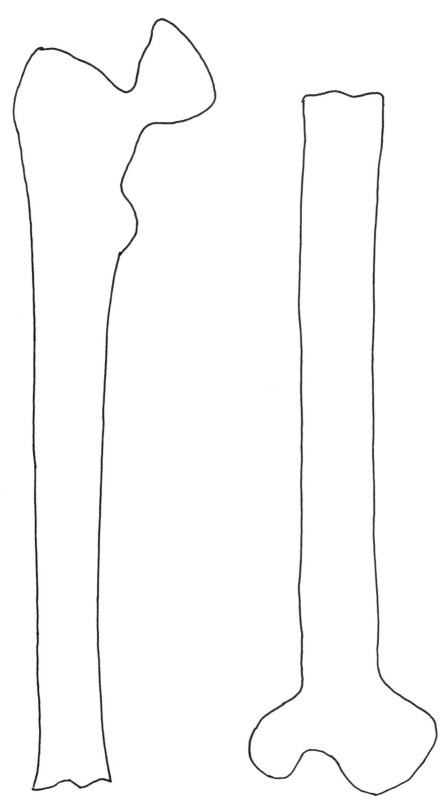

Worksheet A

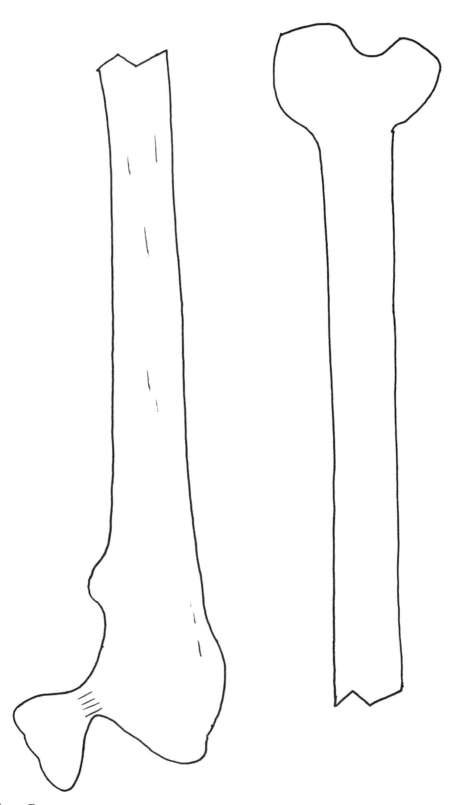

Worksheet B

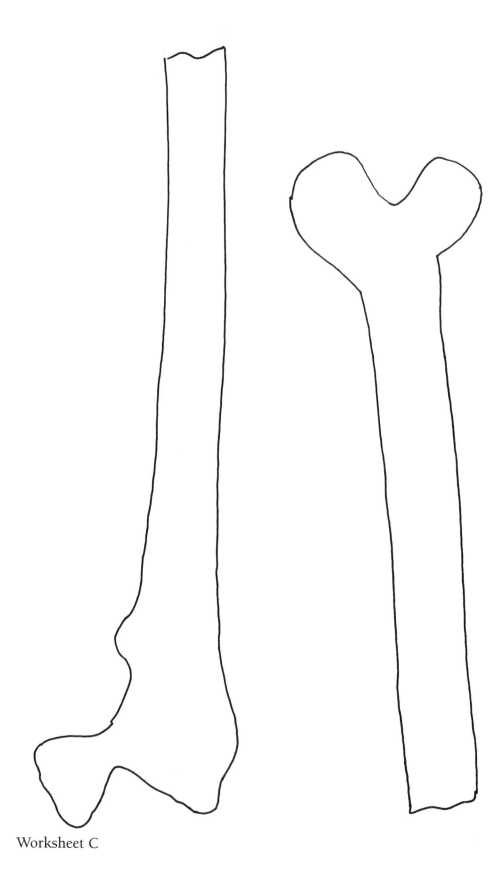

Worksheet C

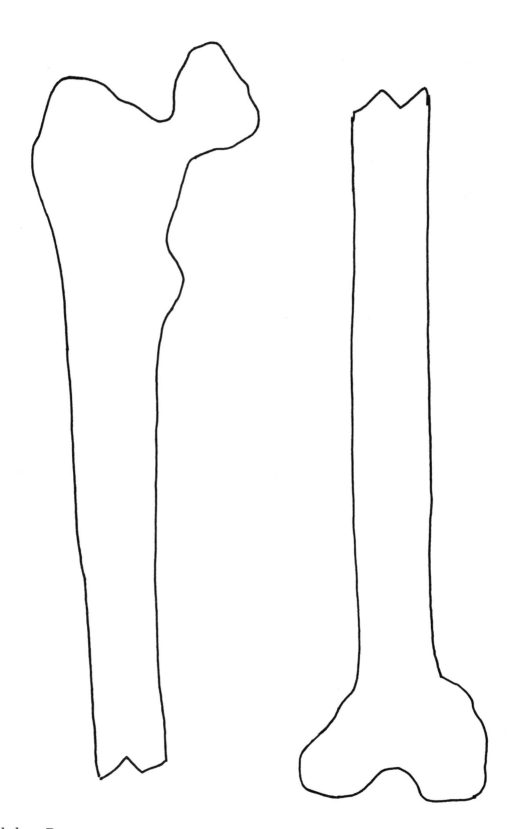

Worksheet D

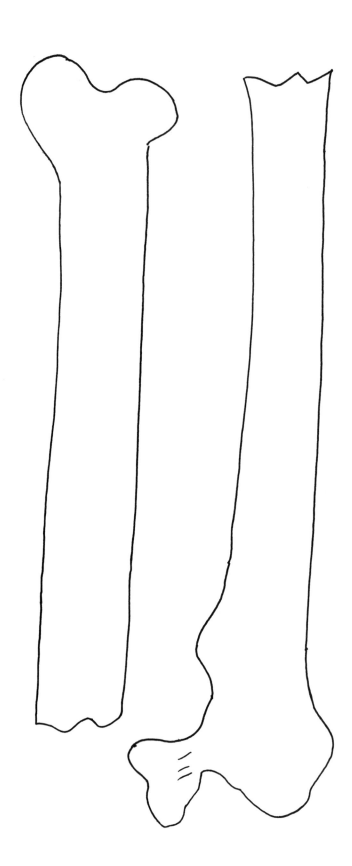

Worksheet E

DATA TABLE 1. LENGTH OF FEMURS.	
Femur	**Length in cm**
A	
B	
C	
D	
E	

The femur is located between the knee and the pelvis.

Conclusion Questions

1. Use the following formula to determine the height of the owners of the five bones. Show your work and record your answers in Data Table 2.

length of femur (cm) $\times$ 2.6 + 65 = height of individual

DATA TABLE 2.		
Femur	**Demonstration of Work**	**Answer in cm**
A		
B		
C		
D		
E		

2. Based on the information given in the Background and your answers in Conclusion Question 1, which femur belongs to the Pharaoh?

_____

_____

_____

3. Which of the individuals was the shortest person?

_____

_____

_____

4. Would you expect *your* own femur to be as long as any of the femurs you measured in the investigation? Explain your answer.

_____

_____

_____

5. Write a memo (5–10 sentences) to the Roth Museum explaining your findings. In the memo, include a description of the method you used to determine the Pharaoh's identity. (You should assume that the museum owner does not understand what is meant by the term "femur.")

_____

_____

_____

_____

_____

_____

_____

_____

_____

INVESTIGATION 3–6

ONE BITE TOO MANY

TEACHER INFORMATION

When a school is vandalized, police find a half-eaten apple near the crime scene. Students help the police investigate by comparing teeth impressions in the apple to mold impressions of three suspects' teeth.

Investigation Objective:

Compare teeth marks from a crime scene bite mold with bite molds from three suspects.

Time Required: 50 minutes

Notes for the Teacher:

1. Read the Background to students, then have them read The Crime. Photocopy Figure 24 and Figure 25 from the Background for your students to use as you read the material to them.

2. Copy the Student Investigator Page for each student or for each group of students. This activity is best done in groups of 2 or 3 students.

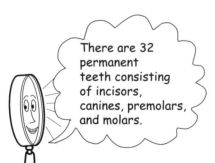

There are 32 permanent teeth consisting of incisors, canines, premolars, and molars.

3. A day or more before the investigation, get three people to bite into a thick piece of plasticine or clay. Be sure they bite down so there is an impression on both the top and bottom of the clay. Two people should give you eight bite molds in eight different pieces of plasticine. One person should give you 16 bite molds. Clean each bite mold with dilute bleach.

4. Label all eight bite molds from one person as "A," all eight from another person as "B," and 8 of the 16 remaining bite molds as "C." Label the eight molds that remain as "Crime Scene."

167

5. The morning of the lab place all the "A" bite molds in a group, the "B" in a group, the "C" in a group, and the "Crime Scene" in a group on the front table.

6. Explain to students that the Crime Scene bite mold was made by a dentist from an apple at the scene of the crime. The other three molds came from the three suspects. Students are to determine which suspect (if any) was involved in the crime.

7. Make sure the students understand figures 24 and 25 before beginning the activity.

Background:

If someone bit you on the arm, you could match the bite marks on your arm to an imprint of their teeth. Bite-mark evidence has been used to identify individuals and convict criminals. This evidence is useful because everyone's teeth are a little different. An investigator looks for points of similarity between a suspect's teeth and the bite marks at the scene of a crime.

Over the years, chewing gradually wears down portions of your teeth. Some people even chip or crack their teeth. Dental fillings also make surfaces of teeth unique.

Your teeth are not all the same shape and size because each tooth has a special function (figures 24 and 25). On both the upper and lower jaw in the front of your mouth are four teeth called incisors; they are made for biting. Beside the incisors are long, sharp canine teeth; canines are made for tearing. In back of the canines are two teeth called premolars. Each premolar has two projections or points that are designed to cut food. Behind the premolars are three molar teeth. These are used to grind food and, therefore, have a fairly smooth surface. There are a total of 32 permanent teeth; 16 on the top of the mouth and 16 on the bottom.

Materials:

Clay (plasticine)
Bite-mark molds from Suspect A, B, C, and crime scene

Answers to Conclusion Questions of Investigation 3–6:

1. Suspect C. There were more points of similarity between C's bite mold and the crime-scene bite mold.

2. Answers will vary.

3. Answers will vary.

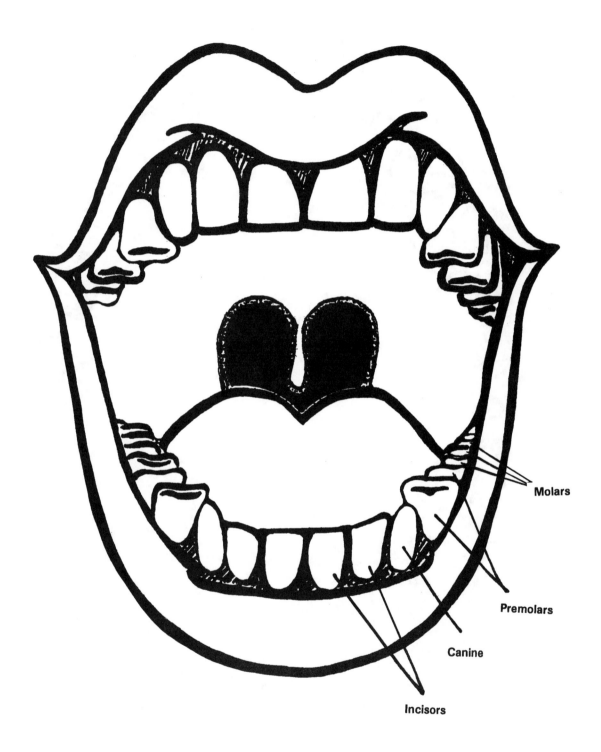

Figure 24. The different types of teeth.

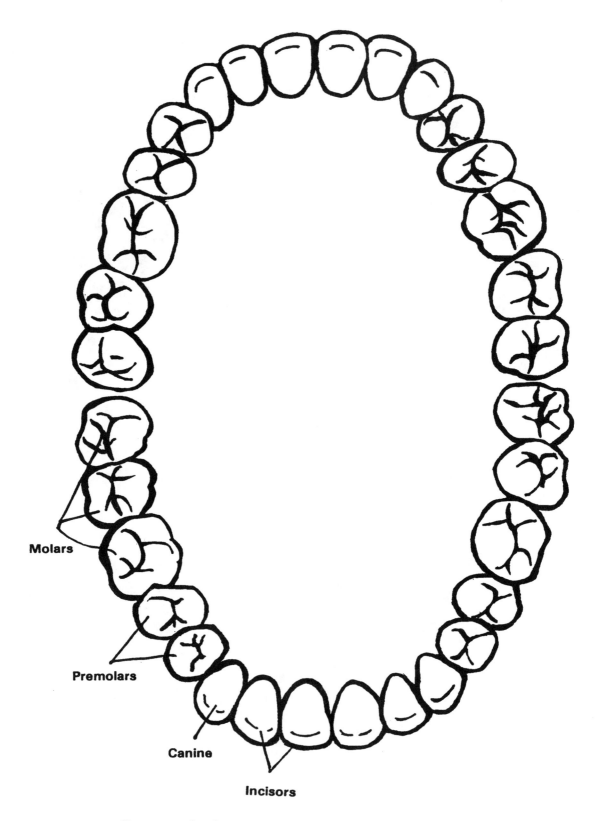

Molars

Premolars

Canine

Incisors

Figure 25. Different types of teeth.

NSTA Objectives that apply to this investigation

As a result of activities in grades K–4, all students should develop:

- abilities necessary to do scientific inquiry and understanding about scientific inquiry. Students should use data to construct a reasonable explanation. (*Elementary Standard, Science as Inquiry*)

- an understanding of characteristics of organisms, life cycle of organisms, and organisms and the environment. Students should recognize that each plant or animal has different structures that serve different functions in growth, survival, and reproduction. (*Elementary Standard, Life Science*)

As a result of activities in grades 5–8, all students should develop:

- abilities necessary to do scientific inquiry and understanding about scientific inquiry. Students should understand fundamental concepts and principles that underlie the understanding about the abilities necessary to do scientific inquiry. Students should think critically and logically to make the relationships between evidence and explanations. Students should be able to review data from a simple experiment, summarize the data, and form a logical argument about the cause-and-effect relationships in the experiment. (*Grades 5–8 Standard, Science as Inquiry*)

- understanding of structure and function in living things, reproduction and heredity, regulation and behavior, populations and ecosystems, and diversity and adaptations of organisms. Students should understand fundamental concepts and principles that underlie the understanding of diversity and adaptations of organisms. Biological evolution accounts for the diversity of species developed through gradual processes over many generations. Species acquire many of their unique characteristics through biological adaptation, which involves the selection of naturally occurring variations in populations. Biological adaptations include changes in structures, behaviors, or physiology that enhance survival and reproductive success in a particular environment. (*Grades 5–8 Standard, Life Science*)

- abilities necessary to do scientific inquiry and understanding about scientific inquiry. Students should understand fundamental concepts and principles that underlie the understanding about the abilities necessary to do scientific inquiry. Students should develop descriptions, explanations, predictions, and models using evidence. (*Grades 5–8, Science as Inquiry*)

- understanding of structure and function in living things, reproduction and heredity, regulation and behavior, populations and ecosystems, and diversity and adaptations of organisms. Students should understand fundamental concepts and principles that underlie the understanding of structure and function in living systems. The human organism has systems for digestion, respiration, reproduction, circulation, excretion, movement, control, and coordination, and for protection from disease. These systems interact with one another. (*Grades 5–8 Standard, Life Science*)

Name _____ Date _____

ONE BITE TOO MANY
Student Investigator Page

The Crime

Magnoview Middle School was vandalized last night. At 6:00 A.M. this morning the principal, Mr. Hewitt, discovered graffiti across the front of the building. He and the police searched the campus for clues. No footprints were found, but a partially eaten apple was located near the building. The apple had not yet turned brown, so police feel that it was dropped there recently. The crime scene specialists placed the apple in a plastic bag and labeled it. They rushed the apple sample to crime scene dental experts. These dentists made a mold of the teeth marks in the apple.

Later that day, the principal called all the students to the auditorium. He offered a $50 reward to any student with information that could help solve the graffiti mystery. After the assembly, three students came forward with information. Each of the students blamed a different individual for the crime.

Mr. Hewitt contacted the police and gave them the names of the three people accused by fellow students. Police officers came back to school and questioned the three accused students. All three denied being near the building after school hours last night. The police asked the individuals to participate in a little experiment. Each agreed to give police officers a mold impression of their teeth. Your job is to compare the cast from the apple with the cast made by the three students.

Procedure

1. Obtain a bite sample from students A, B, and C. Pick up a bite sample from the crime scene apple.

There are 32 permanent teeth consisting of incisors, canines, premolars, and molars.

2. Use figures 24 and 25 to help you locate different teeth on the bite molds. In Data Table 1 make notes about the different teeth on the top part of the bite sample and in Data Table 2 make notes about the different teeth on the bottom part of the bite sample.

You should note chipped or missing teeth, worn teeth, gaps in teeth, and other unique features. For example, you might note such things as a chip on incisor 3 or a smooth area on incisor 2.

DATA TABLE 1. TEETH IN UPPER JAW.				
	Crime scene mold	A	B	C
Incisor 1				
Incisor 2				
Incisor 3				
Incisor 4				
Canine Left				
Canine Right				
Premolar 1 (left)				
Premolar 2 (left)				
Premolar 1 (right)				
Premolar 2 (right)				
Molar 1 (left)				
Molar 2 (left)				
Molar 3 (left)				
Molar 1 (right)				
Molar 2 (right)				
Molar 3 (right)				

	Crime scene mold	A	B	C
DATA TABLE 2. TEETH IN LOWER JAW.				
Incisor 1				
Incisor 2				
Incisor 3				
Incisor 4				
Canine Left				
Canine Right				
Premolar 1 (left)				
Premolar 2 (left)				
Premolar 1 (right)				
Premolar 2 (right)				
Molar 1 (left)				
Molar 2 (left)				
Molar 3 (left)				
Molar 1 (right)				
Molar 2 (right)				
Molar 3 (right)				

Conclusion Questions

1. Who was the criminal? Explain your answer.

   _____

   _____

   _____

   _____

   _____

   _____

2. Describe any obvious dental features that helped you rule out any of the three suspects.

   _____

   _____

   _____

   _____

   _____

   _____

3. Write an ending to this mystery. Name your criminal and explain how you arrived at your conclusion. Describe how you can effectively present this case to the parents of the criminal.

   _____

   _____

   _____

   _____

   _____

   _____

   _____

INVESTIGATION 3–7

LEERY OF LABELS

TEACHER INFORMATION

In this investigation, students help a health-conscious consumer determine whether the labels on different brands of margarine labeled "fat-free" are accurate. Like scientists at the Food & Drug Administration, they test each for the presence of oil.

Investigation Objectives:

Test samples of margarine to determine whether or not they contain fat.

Time Required: 40 minutes

Notes for the Teacher:

1. Read the Background to students, then have them read The Crime.

2. Copy the Student Investigator Page for each group or for each student. This activity is best done in groups of 2 or 3.

3. Before the investigation, purchase four kinds of margarine: two that contain fat (or oil) and two that do not.

Fat in the diet has been linked to several diseases.

4. Before class, prepare the oil and butter samples for each lab group:
   - Label five small dishes with each of the five titles:

     Oil

     Trim and Terrific Fat-Free Margarine

     Mama's Fat-Free Margarine

     Fat-Buster Margarine

     Unbelievably Not Fat Margarine
   - In the dish labeled "Oil," place a few drops of oil.
   - In the dish labeled "Trim and Terrific Fat-Free Margarine," place a small amount of margarine containing oil.

■ In the dish labeled "Mama's Fat-Free Margarine," place a small amount of another brand of margarine that contains oil.

■ In the dish labeled "Fat-Buster Margarine," place a small amount of margarine that does not contain oil.

■ In the dish labeled "Unbelievably Not Fat Margarine," place a small amount of another brand of margarine that does not contain oil.

Background:

The Food and Drug Administration (FDA) is a federal agency that regulates the ingredients in foods, medicines, cosmetics, and other consumer items. FDA scientists try to make sure that these products are safe and that they contain the ingredients their labels say they contain. If the FDA receives complaints about a specific product, they will investigate it.

Since "fat-free" foods have been introduced to the market, consumers are buying them in large quantities. Fat in the diet has been linked to several diseases. Fat and oil are similar in many ways. Most fats come from animals, whereas oils are made from plants. Consequently, many people eat a very low-fat (and low-oil) diet.

Materials:

Oil sample
Trim and Terrific Fat-Free Margarine sample
Mama's Fat-Free Margarine sample
Fat-Buster Margarine sample
Unbelievably Not Fat Margarine sample
Brown paper bag
Scissors
5 cotton swabs

Answers to Conclusion Questions of Investigation 3–7:

1. They test foods, drugs, cosmetics, and other products to determine if they are safe, and if they contain the ingredients they claim to contain.

2. An oil or fat creates a translucent area on brown paper.

3. 3

4. The Fat-Buster Margarine and Unbelievably Not Fat Margarine. They did not cause a translucent spot on brown paper.

5. Answers may vary. The oil was a control and it demonstrated a known positive test.

6. Obesity and some diseases have been linked to large amounts of fat in the diet.

7. Answers will vary.

NSTA Objectives that apply to this investigation

As a result of activities in grades K–4, all students should develop:

- abilities necessary to do scientific inquiry and understanding about scientific inquiry. Students should employ simple equipment and tools to gather data and extend the senses. Students should use data to construct a reasonable explanation. (*Elementary Standard, Science as Inquiry*)

- an understanding of characteristics of organisms, life cycle of organisms, and organisms and the environment. Students should understand fundamental concepts and principles that underlie the properties of organisms and their environment. Humans depend on their natural and construct environment. Humans change environments in ways that can be either beneficial or detrimental for themselves and other organisms. (*Elementary Standard, Life Science*)

- abilities of technological design, understanding about science and technology, and abilities to distinguish between natural objects and objects made by humans. Students should understand fundamental concepts and principles that underlie the understanding about science and technology. People have always had problems and invented tools and techniques to solve problems. Trying to determine the effects of solutions helps people avoid some new problems. (*Elementary Standard, Science and Technology*)

- abilities of technological design, understanding about science and technology, and abilities to distinguish between natural objects and objects made by humans. Students should understand fundamental concepts and principles that underlie the understanding about science and technology. Tools help scientists make better observations, measurements, and equipment for investigations. They help scientists see, measure, and do things that they could not otherwise see, measure, and do. (*Elementary Standard, Science and Technology*)

- understanding of personal health, characteristics and changes in population, types of resources, changes in environments, and science and technology in local challenges. Students should understand fundamental concepts and principles that underlie the understanding about science and technology in local challenges. Science and technology have greatly improved food quality and quantity, transportation, health, sanitation, and communication. These benefits of science and technology are not available to all of the people in the world. (*Elementary Standard, Science in Personal and Social Perspectives*)

As a result of activities in grades 5–8, all students should develop:

- abilities necessary to do scientific inquiry and understandings about scientific inquiry. Students should use appropriate tools and techniques to gather, analyze, and interpret data. Students should think critically and logically to make the relationships between evidence and explanations. (*Grades 5–8 Standard, Science as Inquiry*)

■ abilities necessary to do scientific inquiry and understandings about scientific inquiry. Students should understand fundamental concepts and principles that underlie the understanding about the abilities necessary to do scientific inquiry. Students should think critically and logically to make the relationships between evidence and explanations. Students should be able to review data from a simple experiment, summarize the data, and form a logical argument about the cause-and-effect relationships in the experiment. (*Grades 5–8 Standard, Science as Inquiry*)

Name _____ Date _____

LEERY OF LABELS
Student Investigator Page

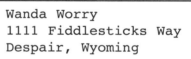

The Crime

"Fat-free" foods are all over the grocery store, from the meat department to the ice cream freezer. Many people avoid eating a lot of fat and oil for several reasons: Fat and oil in the diet are linked to heart disease and other health problems. They also cause weight gain more easily than other types of food.

One of the FDA scientists, Terry Testtube, received the following letter from a lady named Wanda Worry. He has decided to check out her complaint and let her know what he discovers.

Wanda Worry
1111 Fiddlesticks Way
Despair, Wyoming

Dear Mr. Testtube,

I read about you and the other FDA scientists in the newspaper. I see that your job is to make sure that the ingredient labels on products are accurate. Well, I think I've found some that are incorrect.

I'm trying to lose weight, so I eat a lot of fat-free foods. My favorite food in the world is margarine, and I put it on everything. Since I've been on my diet, I haven't lost a pound. I'm beginning to think that those fat-free margarines must really contain some fat. That's false advertising, and it could be dangerous. Would you check the following brands of margarine to see if they are really fat-free?

> Trim and Terrific Fat-Free Margarine
> Mama's Fat-Free Margarine
> Fat-Buster Margarine
> Unbelievably Not Fat Margarine

Thanks for your help. I'm anxiously awaiting your reply.

Sincerely,
Wanda

Procedure

Fat in the diet has been linked to several diseases.

1. Cut part of the brown paper bag into five pieces about the size of your hand. Label these pieces as "Oil,""Trim and Terrific Fat-Free Margarine," "Mama's Fat-Free Margarine," "Fat-Buster Margarine," and "Unbelievably Not Fat Margarine."

2. Demonstrate a positive test for oil (or fat):

   a. Dip one of the cotton swabs in the oil sample.

   b. Rub the oily swab over the piece of brown paper labeled "Oil."

   c. Notice that the oily spot becomes translucent. This means that light can pass through it. This area on the brown paper is a positive test for fat or oil. Indicate this on the Data Table.

3. Test the "Trim and Terrific Fat-Free Margarine" for the presence of oil. Dip a swab in the sample, then rub it over the appropriate piece of brown paper. Hold the paper up to the light to see if it is translucent. If it is, indicate this in the Data Table.

4. Repeat step 3 for the other margarine samples. Record all results in the Data Table.

DATA TABLE. RESULTS OF FAT (OIL) TEST ON MARGARINE SAMPLES.		
Margarine sample	**Translucent on brown paper? (yes or no)**	**Contains oil or fat? (yes or no)**
Oil		
Trim and Terrific		
Mama's Fat-Free		
Fat-Buster		
Unbelievably Not Fat		

Conclusion Questions

1. What is the job of some of the scientists employed by the FDA?

   _____

   _____

   _____

   _____

2. What is a positive test for oil or fat in a substance?

   _____

   _____

   _____

   _____

3. Including the oil sample, how many of the samples that you tested contained oil?

   _____

   _____

   _____

   _____

4. Which of the samples that you tested as fat-free margarine products were actually fat free? How do you know?

   _____

   _____

   _____

   _____

5. Why did you rub a sample of oil on a piece of paper?

   _____

   _____

   _____

   _____

6. Why do people need to know if their food contains oil and fat?

   _____

   _____

   _____

   _____

7. On another sheet of paper, write a letter to Wanda explaining your test results.

INVESTIGATION 3–8
DNA NET

TEACHER INFORMATION

During the night Tom's car is stolen and found wrecked a few miles away, with a trace of blood on the steering wheel. To help the police, students simulate running a DNA match on the suspects by using a reproducible bar code worksheet in place of real DNA screens.

Investigation Objectives:

Compare DNA evidence from different individuals.

Use DNA evidence to identify a criminal.

Time Required: 50 minutes

Notes for the Teacher:

1. Read the Background to students, then have them read The Crime.

2. Photocopy Figures 26 and 27 from the Background, the Bar Code Worksheet, and the Student Investigator Page for each group or for each student. This activity is best done in groups of 2 or 3.

3. Discuss the importance of DNA and where it is found. Emphasize that each person's DNA is unique. You may want to mention some well-known court cases that have relied on DNA evidence.

Except for identical twins, everyone's DNA is unique.

Background:

DNA evidence can be used by detectives to help solve crimes. DNA is found in every cell of your body. Each person's cells differ from everyone else's because everyone has different DNA. In other words, DNA in your cells makes you unique. The only people who have the same DNA are identical twins.

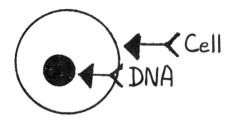

Figure 26. DNA is found in each cell.

You can compare DNA samples from two people and see that they are different. You can collect DNA from cells such as skin, blood, and other body fluids. After the DNA is removed from the cells, it is placed in a device that separates it into its parts. These parts look much like the lines in a bar code. You may have seen bar codes on food packages and other purchases in your home.

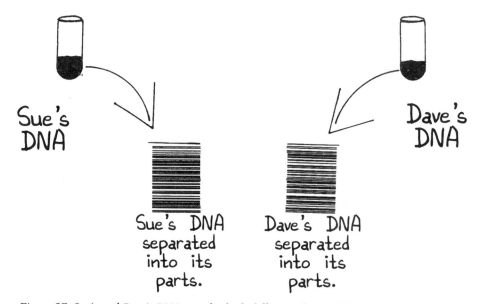

Figure 27. Sue's and Dave's DNA samples look different after each has been separated into its parts.

Materials:

Bar code worksheets
Scissors

Answers to Conclusion Questions of Investigation 3–8:

1. one; Ima Isuzu

2. DNA evidence

3. no; identical twins have the same DNA

4. blood on the steering wheel

5. skin or body fluids

6. Answers will vary.

NSTA Objectives that apply to this investigation

As a result of activities in grades K–4, all students should develop:

■ abilities necessary to do scientific inquiry and understanding about scientific inquiry. Students should employ simple equipment and tools to gather data and extend the senses. Students should use data to construct a reasonable explanation. (*Elementary Standard, Science as Inquiry*)

■ an understanding of characteristics of organisms, life cycle of organisms, and organisms and the environment. Students should understand fundamental concepts and principles that underlie the properties of life cycles of organisms. Plants and animals closely resemble their parents. (*Elementary Standard, Life Science*)

■ abilities of technological design, understanding about science and technology, and abilities to distinguish between natural objects and objects made by humans. Students should understand fundamental concepts and principles that underlie the understanding about science and technology. Tools help scientists make better observations, measurements, and equipment for investigations. They help scientists see, measure, and do things that they could not otherwise see, measure, and do. (*Elementary Standard, Science and Technology*)

As a result of activities in grades 5–8, all students should develop:

■ understanding of structure and function in living things, reproduction and heredity, regulation and behavior, populations and ecosystems, and diversity and adaptations of organisms. Students should understand fundamental concepts and principles that underlie the understanding of diversity and adaptations of organisms. Biological evolution accounts for the diversity of species developed through gradual processes over many generations. Species acquire many of their unique characteristics through biological adaptation, which involves the selection of naturally occurring variations in populations. Biological adaptations include changes in structures, behaviors, or physiology that enhance survival and reproductive success in a particular environment. (*Grades 5–8 Standard, Life Science*)

■ abilities necessary to do scientific inquiry and understandings about scientific inquiry. Students should understand fundamental concepts and principles that underlie the understanding about the abilities necessary to do scientific inquiry. Students should think critically and logically to make the relationships between evidence and explanations. Students should be able to review data from a simple experiment, summarize the data, and form a logical argument about the cause-and-effect relationships in the experiment. (*Grades 5–8 Standard, Science as Inquiry*)

■ abilities necessary to do scientific inquiry and understandings about scientific inquiry. Students should understand fundamental concepts and principles that underlie the understanding about the abilities necessary to do scientific inquiry. Students should develop descriptions, explanations, predictions, and models using evidence. (*Grades 5–8, Science as Inquiry*)

■ understanding of structure and function in living things, reproduction and heredity, regulation and behavior, populations and ecosystems, and diversity and adaptations of organisms. Students should understand fundamental concepts and principles that underlie the understanding of reproduction and heredity. Hereditary information is contained in genes, located in the chromosomes of each cell. Each gene carries a single unit of information. A human cell contains many thousands of different genes. (*Grades 5–8 Standard, Life Science*)

Name _____ Date _____

DNA Net
Student Investigator Page

The Crime

Tom lives in a community surrounded by a security gate. Jim and his employees monitor the gate 24 hours a day. Only residents and guests with special passes are allowed through the gate. Saturday night Tom waved to Jim as he entered the gate at 10:00 P.M. Sunday morning Tom was enjoying a quiet breakfast at home when the police knocked on his door. A police officer reported that Tom's vehicle had been found several miles away. The car was a total wreck and blood was found on the steering wheel.

After talking with Jim at the gate, the police realized that no visitors had passed through the gate after 10:00 P.M. Saturday night. Therefore, it was decided that a resident of the apartment complex was responsible for the theft.

Police carried out a DNA search. This means that the police took samples of DNA from all residents of Tom's apartment complex. They also took DNA from the blood found on Tom's steering wheel. Once the tests were completed, they compared the DNA from the steering wheel with the DNA samples from the residents.

Procedure

1. Use scissors to cut out the bar code that represents the DNA sample from the crime scene.

2. Compare this crime scene sample with the bar codes of residents from Tom's apartment complex.

3. Determine which resident's bar code matches the crime scene bar code.

Except for identical twins, everyone's DNA is unique.

The Bar Code Worksheet

These bar codes represent DNA evidence from the crime scene and from each resident of Tom's apartment building.

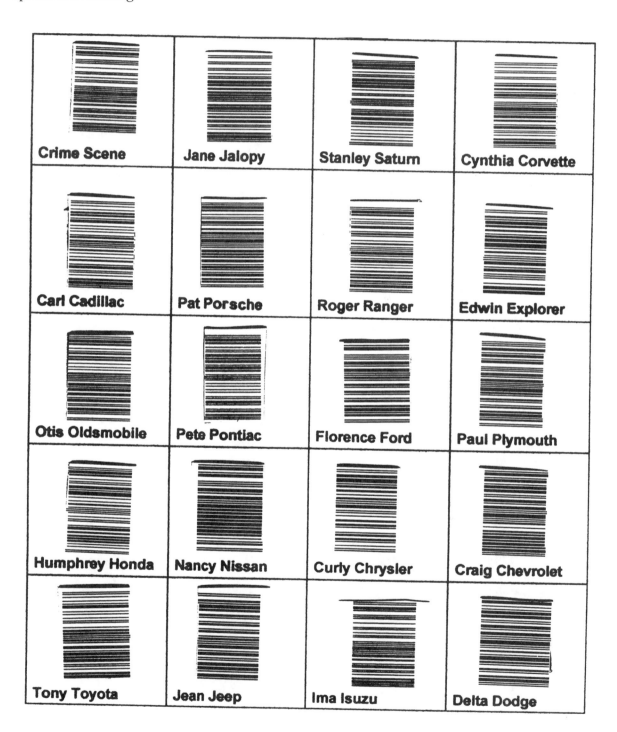

Conclusion Questions

1. How many residents of Tom's apartment complex matched the crime scene bar code?_____
   List the names of all matches.

   _____

   _____

2. What do the bar codes in this activity represent?

   _____

   _____

3. Jane and Julie are identical twins. If police found that one of these two girls had committed
   a crime, could they determine which one is guilty based on their DNA samples?

   _____ Why or why not? _____

   _____

   _____

4. Police officers obtained DNA samples from Tom's vehicle. What evidence left by the criminal provided the DNA sample?

   _____

   _____

5. Besides the answer given to question 4, suggest other sources of DNA that might be left at
   a crime scene.

   _____

   _____

   _____

6. Write a one-paragraph story that describes a crime in which DNA was collected and used
   as evidence.

   _____

   _____

   _____

   _____

   _____

SECTION 4

PHYSICAL SCIENCE

INVESTIGATION 4-1

WHERE IS HERMAN THE HAMSTER?

TEACHER INFORMATION

When a school is robbed, a teacher's pet hamster, Herman, disappears. Students can help find Herman by making a rough sketch of the crime scene. They must sharpen their observation skills and make careful measurements to solve this one.

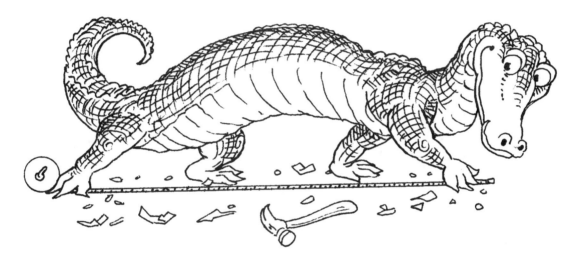

Investigation Objectives:

Observe a crime scene.
Draw a rough sketch of the crime scene.

Time Required: 50 minutes

Don't touch or move any objects when you enter the room!

Notes for the Teacher:

1. Read the Background to your students, then have them read The Crime.

2. Copy the Student Investigator Page and Figure 28 for each student. This activity is best done individually.

3. If students are not familiar with metric units, you should review how to read a metric ruler. Their measurements in this investigation will be made using centimeters. You may want to remind students that 2.54 cm

equals 1 inch. This would mean a 6-foot-tall (72-inch) man would be about 183 cm tall. This will give students a relationship between cm and inches.

4. Discuss with students the importance of good observation skills in crime scene investigations.

5. The day before the activity, arrange the crime scene. Select a room that is ordinarily not used in the school or one that you can use for your activity the next day. Go in the room and turn over some desks and chairs. Place some unusual items around the room, such as a tube of lipstick, a pet collar (Herman's), an earring, an old test with a student's name on it, a hat, a grocery store receipt, a pay stub, etc. Be original. If possible, place yellow tape or yellow construction paper labeled "Crime Scene—Do Not Enter" at the entrance to the door.

Background:

The clues to solving a crime are often found at the crime scene. The first police officer at the scene of a crime must rope off the area to prevent damage that may occur to evidence. The crime scene investigator takes notes about the area. This written information must be exact since it may be used in a future trial.

Photography, sketches, and notes are three ways the crime scene is recorded. Sketches and notes by the investigators are very important records. First, "rough" sketches of the crime scene are made. These sketches include the location of important objects in the room. The rough sketch will show all physical evidence and other important features (Figure 28).

In the sketches, objects are labeled in relation to two fixed points in a room. The two fixed points may be two walls of a room. A tape measure is used to find the exact length and width of the room and distances of key objects from two fixed points. A compass is used to orient the room to North and South. A good crime scene sketch will allow the person looking at it to feel as if he or she is actually at the location.

Materials

Metric measuring tape
White unlined paper
Ruler
Pencil
Compass

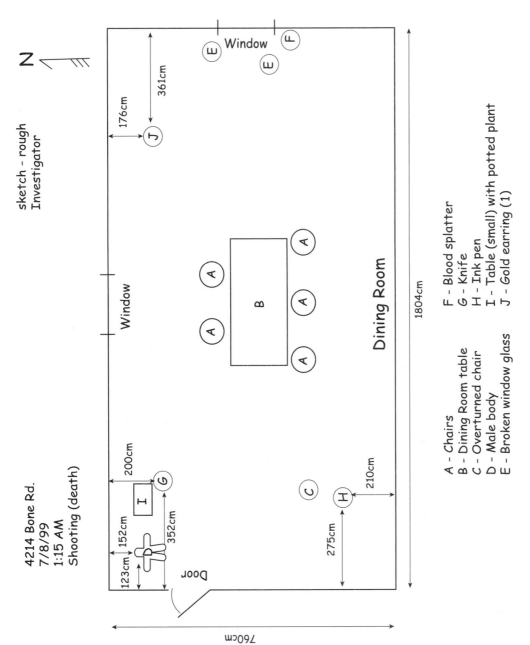

Figure 28. Rough sketch made by investigator at a shooting that occurred on Bone Road. Notice objects are labeled on the sketch and distances are included. For example, an ink pen was sketched in relation to the two adjacent walls of the room.

Answers to Conclusion Questions of Investigation 4–1:

1. to protect the evidence
2. fixed points
3. photographing and making notes
4. Answers will vary depending on the crime scene.
5. Answers will vary.

NSTA Objectives that apply to this investigation

As a result of activities in grades K–4, all students should develop:

- abilities necessary to do scientific inquiry and understanding about scientific inquiry. Students should use data to construct a reasonable explanation. (*Elementary Standard, Science as Inquiry*)

- abilities necessary to do scientific inquiry and understanding about scientific inquiry. Students should communicate investigations and explanations. This communication might be spoken or drawn as well as written. (*Elementary Standard, Science as Inquiry*)

- an understanding of properties of objects and materials, position and motion of objects, light, heat, electricity, and magnetism. Students should understand fundamental concepts and principles that underlie the properties of position and motion of objects. The position of an object can be described by locating it relative to another object or background. (*Elementary Standard, Physical Science*)

- abilities of technological design, understanding about science and technology, and abilities to distinguish between natural objects and objects made by humans. Students should understand fundamental concepts and principles that underlie the understanding about science and technology. Tools help scientists make better observations, measurements, and equipment for investigations. They help scientists see, measure, and do things that they could not otherwise see, measure, and do. (*Elementary Standard, Science and Technology*)

As a result of activities in grades 5–8, all students should develop:

- abilities necessary to do scientific inquiry and understandings about scientific inquiry. Students should use appropriate tools and techniques to gather, analyze, and interpret data. Students should think critically and logically to make the relationships between evidence and explanations. (*Grades 5–8 Standard, Science as Inquiry*)

- abilities necessary to do scientific inquiry and understandings about scientific inquiry. Students should understand fundamental concepts and principles that underlie the understanding about the abilities necessary to do scientific inquiry. Students should think critically and logically to make the relationships between evidence and explanations. Students should be able to review data from a simple experiment, summarize the data, and form a logical argument about the cause-and-effect relationships in the experiment. (*Grades 5–8 Standard, Science as Inquiry*)

- abilities necessary to do scientific inquiry and understandings about scientific inquiry. Students should understand fundamental concepts and principles that underlie the understanding about the abilities necessary to do scientific inquiry. Students should use mathematics in all aspects of scientific inquiry. Mathematics can be used to ask questions; to gather, organize, and present data; and to structure convincing explanations. (*Grades 5–8, Science as Inquiry*)

Name _____ Date _____

WHERE IS HERMAN THE HAMSTER?
STUDENT INVESTIGATOR PAGE

The Crime

Last night, the school was robbed and vandalized. In Mr. Simpson's classroom, several desks were turned over. Officers roped off the room to protect any evidence in it. It has been left undisturbed all day.

Mr. Simpson reported that one very valuable object was missing. The pet hamster, Herman, was nowhere to be found. Mr. Simpson's class is anxious to locate Herman because Herman is a very finicky eater. He will not eat when strangers are near. It is feared Herman may starve before the hamster thief can be found. You can help find Herman by making a rough sketch of the crime scene. Authorities will use your sketch as evidence.

Procedure

1. Accompany your teacher to the scene of the crime.

2. When you enter the room, be careful not to touch or move any objects.

3. Using Figure 28 as an example, on unlined white paper make a rough sketch of the crime scene. It should include the following:

   a. Length and width of the room in centimeters (cm).

   b. Placement of windows and doors. Label windows and doors with a letter. At the bottom of the sketch, create a key that explains your labels.

   c. Orientation to the North.

   d. Placement of desks, chairs, tables, and other furniture. Let circles represent desks and chairs. Let rectangles represent the pieces of large furniture, such as tables. Use a letter to label each. Include these labels in your key.

   e. Placement of out-of-place or unusual items (example: scarves, necklaces, earrings, cash receipts, wallets, etc.). Let circles represent out-of-place items. Also label these items with a letter. Include these labels in your key.

Don't touch or move any objects when you enter the room!

f. For each unusual item that you drew in the sketch, select two fixed points near that item. Label each fixed point with an arrow. Measure the distance of each unusual object from each fixed point and record that on your sketch.

g. Write the date, time, description of crime scene, crime, your name, school location, and room number at the top of the sketch.

Conclusion Questions

1. Why is a crime scene roped off when it is first found?

   _____

   _____

2. When you sketch objects in a crime scene, each object is measured from two

   _____   _____.

3. Beside sketching, what are two other ways to record a crime scene?

   _____

   _____

4. List all the objects that were unusual or out of place at the crime scene you observed today.

   _____

   _____

   _____

   _____

5. Write a paragraph that explains Herman's disappearance. Base your story on what you saw at the crime scene. Be creative and explain whether or not Herman was found in time. What led investigators to solve this mystery?

   _____

   _____

   _____

   _____

   _____

   _____

   _____

   _____

INVESTIGATION 4–2

CANDY CAPERS

TEACHER INFORMATION

This could be a tasty investigation! Students help Mrs. McFarland find out who's been eating candy in her class by preparing chromatograms of the food dye in two different types of candy.

Investigation Objectives:

Separate water-soluble food dye into colors. Compare the crime scene candy colors with the known candy colors.

Time Required: 50 minutes

Notes for the Teacher:

1. Read the Background to students, then have them read The Crime.

2. Copy the Student Investigator Page for each student or for each group of students. This activity is best done in groups of 2 or 3 students.

3. The day before the investigation, prepare a chromatogram of the dye on Skittles® candy for each group. This chromatogram will serve as the Crime Scene napkin. *To prepare this chromatogram:* On a piece of filter paper, coffee filter, or paper napkin, dampen and rub one of the candies (it doesn't matter what color) across the middle of the paper. Make sure that dye from the candy is on the paper. Spread the paper over a small empty bowl, and secure in place with a rubber band. One drop at a time, add water to the candy stain. Continue to add water until the stain has spread in all directions, and colors of the dye are observed. Figure 29 shows a crime scene chromatogram for one of the investigation groups.

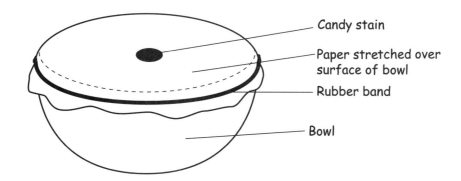

Figure 29. Make a crime scene chromatogram for each investigation group. Rub the dye from a Skittles® candy on a napkin or piece of filter paper. Secure the paper across an open bowl with a rubber band. Center the candy dye in the middle of the bowl.

4. The day of the lab, place some Skittles® candies in a plastic bag and label as "Sample 1." Place some M & M's® in another plastic bag and label as "Sample 2." These will represent the samples the teacher found under the desk in The Crime.

Background:

Dyes are used to color everything from fabrics to food. The interesting colors of dyes are made by mixing basic dye colors. In other words, a dye is a mixture. To separate a dye into its individual colors, you need a liquid that will dissolve that dye. In the case of food dyes, that liquid is water.

A water-soluble food dye can be separated into its individual colors using water as the solvent. To separate a dye, place a spot of it on a strip of filter paper. Some colors in the dye dissolve easily in water and travel quickly up the filter paper. As a result, the colors in the food dye will be separated along the strip of filter paper.

Many types of candy contain water-soluble dyes. These dyes can be used in foods because the United States Food and Drug Administration approves their safety. A special list called the GRAS (generally recognized as safe) list notes which dyes are approved for use in foods.

Materials:

Crime scene napkin
2 brands of hard colored candy
Napkins or filter paper
2 large beakers
Water
Crayons
White unlined paper
Metric ruler

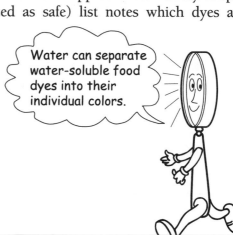

Answers to Conclusion Questions of Investigation 4–2:

1. by mixing basic dye colors

2. A chromatogram is a piece of paper showing the different colors in a dye.

3. Sample 1

4. dark colors

5. Students staple their chromatograms to the paper.

NSTA Objectives that apply to this investigation

As a result of activities in grades K–4, all students should develop:

- abilities necessary to do scientific inquiry and understanding about scientific inquiry. Students should use data to construct a reasonable explanation. (*Elementary Standard, Science as Inquiry*)

As a result of activities in grades 5–8, all students should develop:

- abilities necessary to do scientific inquiry and understandings about scientific inquiry. Students should understand fundamental concepts and principles that underlie the understanding about the abilities necessary to do scientific inquiry. Students should think critically and logically to make the relationships between evidence and explanations. Students should be able to review data from a simple experiment, summarize the data, and form a logical argument about the cause-and-effect relationships in the experiment. (*Grades 5–8 Standard, Science as Inquiry*)

- an understanding of science as a human endeavor, nature of science, and history of science. Students should understand fundamental concepts and principles that underlie the understanding of science as a human endeavor. Some scientists work in teams and some work alone, but all communicate extensively with others. (*Grades 5–8 Standard, History and Nature of Science*)

- abilities necessary to do scientific inquiry and understandings about properties and changes of properties in matter, motions and forces, and transfer of energy. Students should understand fundamental concepts and principles that underlie the properties and changes of properties in matter. A substance has characteristic properties, such as density, boiling point, and solubility, all of which are independent of the amount of the sample. A mixture of substances often can be separated into the original substances using one or more of the characteristic properties. (*Grades 5–8 Standard, Physical Science*)

Name _____ Date _____

CANDY CAPERS

STUDENT INVESTIGATOR PAGE

The Crime

Mrs. McFarland teaches 6th grade science. She does not allow her students to eat candy during class. At recess one day, Mrs. McFarland finds a napkin on the floor that is stained with streaks of color. It seems that someone enjoyed a candy snack before recess.

While students are outside, Mrs. McFarland notices a bag of hard colored candy beside two desks. Mrs. McFarland concludes that one of these two students was eating candy during class. When the students return to class, she asks if the owners of the candy will agree to participate in a simple experiment. Both students agree and give Mrs. McFarland several pieces of candy from their bag. This experiment will determine which of the two types of candy yielded stains on the napkins.

Procedure

1. Examine the crime scene napkin, or chromatogram, provided by your teacher. In Data Table 1, draw and color the chromatogram. Also write the colors on the napkin, in the order they appear, in Data Table 1.

2. Prepare chromatograms for the two types of candy:

   a. Cut 12 strips of filter paper that are 20 cm long and 3 cm wide (Figure 30).

   Figure 30. Strips of filter paper.

   b. Use a ruler and measure two centimeters from the point of each filter paper strip. Draw a straight line in pencil at this point (Figure 31).

Pencil mark

2cm

Figure 31. Draw a pencil line at the pointed end of filter paper strips.

c. Remove one candy of each color from Suspect 1's bag of candy.

d. Take six pieces of filter paper and at the end opposite the pencil line, record a candy color (example: red, green, yellow). See Figure 32.

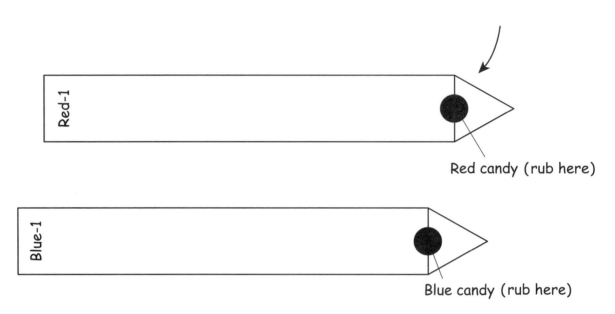

Figure 32. Recording candy colors from Sample 1 candies.

e. Dampen each piece of candy with water and rub the candy on the pencil line. Rub the green candy on the strip marked "green," red on strip marked "red," etc.

f. Place enough water in one beaker to cover the bottom of the beaker.

g. Hang the filter paper strips over the top of the container so that the pointed end just contacts the water. Fold the strip over or tape in place. Do this for all Sample 1 strips (Figure 33).

h. Allow water to travel up the strips until it has dampened most of the strips.

i. Remove the strips and tape them in place on a piece of white paper. Label the paper as "Suspect strips from Candy 1."

j. Repeat steps c through i using the candy from Suspect 2's bag. Label these filter paper strips as "Suspect strips from Candy 2."

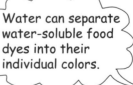

Water can separate water-soluble food dyes into their individual colors.

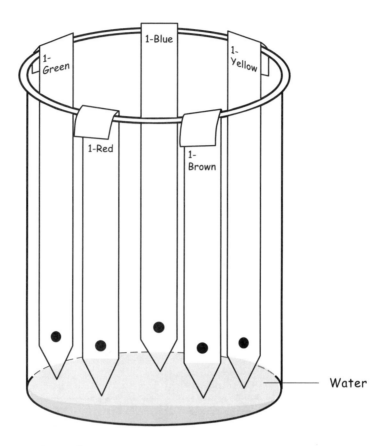

Figure 33. Beaker of water with Sample 1 strips in place.

3. Complete Data Table 2.

DATA TABLE 1. CRIME SCENE CHROMATOGRAM.	
Drawing of crime scene chromatogram	*List of colors in chromatogram*

DATA TABLE 2. CHROMATOGRAMS FROM SUSPECT CANDIES.	
Drawings of Sample 1 chromatograms	*List of colors in each chromatogram*
Drawings of Sample 2 chromatograms	*List of colors in each chromatogram*

Conclusion Questions

1. How are the interesting colors of food dyes made?

    _____

    _____

    _____

    _____

2. What is a chromatogram?

    _____

    _____

    _____

    _____

3. Did candy from Suspect 1 or Suspect 2 form chromatograms that match the stains in the Crime Scene Napkin?

    _____

    _____

4. Which color of candy produced the most different colors?

    _____

    _____

5. Staple your chromatograms to the back of this activity sheet.

INVESTIGATION 4–3
STEPPING INTO CRIME

TEACHER INFORMATION

Bobby and Susy think Jim was trying to steal something from their car, but Bobby says he was attacked by their dog, Jeremiah, for no reason. To see who is telling the truth, students investigate by carefully observing the footprints at the crime scene and make an inference based on their observation. Students are aided by a reproducible page of footprints that they color according to instructions.

Investigation Objectives:

Determine the sequence of events during a crime by analyzing footprints.
Make an inference based on observations.

Time Required: 50 minutes

Notes for the Teacher:

1. Read the Background to your students, then have them read The Crime.

2. Draw Figure 34 on the board and explain how it shows whether footprint A or B was made first.

3. Copy the Student Investigator Page for each student and the "Photograph Page of the Footprints." Collect enough crayons, markers, or colored pencils prior to the lab so each student has access to blue, red, green, yellow, and orange.

Background:

When many different shoe prints are found at a crime scene, the events of the crime can be confusing. An experienced crime scene photographer can make pictures of these prints. All of the resulting photographs can be assembled like puzzle pieces to show the entire crime scene.

Once the crime has been captured on camera, experts can examine the scene and make educated guesses about what happened. When experts look at the footprints in crime scene photographs and take notes, they are making observations. In these notes they indicate things they see in the photograph. An example of an observation is: "Five different sets of footprints are visible on the photograph."

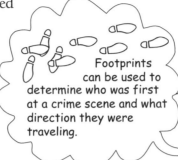

Footprints can be used to determine who was first at a crime scene and what direction they were traveling.

Crime scene experts use these notes to draw some conclusions. Conclusions drawn from evidence are called inferences. An example of an inference is: "Three adults, one dog, and a child were present at the crime scene."

You can learn many things by analyzing footprints. If one person's footprint partially covers another set of prints, you know that the partially covered print was made first (Figure 34). The direction a person or animal was traveling can be determined by observing their footprints.

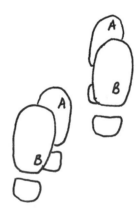

Figure 34. When two prints are located together, you can determine which was made first. In this figure, print A was made prior to print B, so person A was in that location first.

Material:

"Photograph" of footprints from crime scene
Red, blue, yellow, orange, and green crayons

Answers to Conclusion Questions of Investigation 4–3:

1. c—Yellow
   e—Orange
   d—Green
   a—Blue
   b—Red

2. Bobby

3. He gave them to his Mom, Susy, to carry them into the house.

4. No. He went east and west.

5. Yes. Her prints show that Susy followed the dog when he ran from the house.

6. Susy's—

   a. Jim was traveling east first, then turned around at Bobby's and traveled west.

   b. Susy's prints showed that she witnessed the dog's attack.

   c. The dog did not chase Jim; the dog headed Jim off as Jim traveled west.

7. Answers will vary.

NSTA Objectives that apply to this investigation

As a result of activities in grades K–4, all students should develop:

- abilities necessary to do scientific inquiry and understanding about scientific inquiry. Students should employ simple equipment and tools to gather data and extend the senses. Students should use data to construct a reasonable explanation. (*Elementary Standard, Science as Inquiry*)

- abilities necessary to do scientific inquiry and understanding about scientific inquiry. Students should ask a question about objects, organisms, and events in the environment. It is emphasized that students ask questions they can answer with scientific knowledge, combined with their own observations. (*Elementary Standard, Science as Inquiry*)

- an understanding of properties of objects and materials, position and motion of objects, light, heat, electricity, and magnetism. Students should understand fundamental concepts and principles that underlie the properties of position and motion of objects. The position of an object can be described by locating it relative to another object or background. (*Elementary Standard, Physical Science*)

As a result of activities in grades 5–8, all students should develop:

- abilities necessary to do scientific inquiry and understandings about scientific inquiry. Students should understand fundamental concepts and principles that underlie the understanding about the abilities necessary to do scientific inquiry. Students should think critically and logically to make the relationships between evidence and explanations. Students should be able to review data from a simple experiment, summarize the data, and form a logical argument about the cause-and-effect relationships in the experiment. (*Grades 5–8 Standard, Science as Inquiry*)

- abilities necessary to do scientific inquiry and understandings about scientific inquiry. Students should understand fundamental concepts and principles that underlie the understanding about the abilities necessary to do scientific inquiry. Students should develop descriptions, explanations, predictions, and models using evidence. (*Grades 5–8, Science as Inquiry*)

Name _____ **Date** _____

STEPPING INTO CRIME

STUDENT INVESTIGATOR PAGE

The Crime

A crime occurred outside of Bobby Masuda's house last night. Police investigators are trying to determine what actually happened. Jim Starnes claims he was attacked and badly injured near Bobby's property. Bobby's wife, Susy, thinks that Jim was trying to steal something from the trunk of Bobby's car. Susy's and Jim's stories are completely different.

This is the story that Jim told the police:
Last night at 7:00 P.M. I was out for my evening stroll when I was attacked by a German shepherd. I live on the east end of Elm Street. I was walking down Elm from east to west. I was attacked after I passed Bobby's house. Everyone at Bobby's was busy unloading groceries from the car and no one saw the attack.

Susy's story is very different:
Last night at 7:00 Bobby parked the car on the street and got out. He grabbed a few bags of groceries from the trunk and brought them inside. My son, Jesse, and I helped him carry the rest of the bags inside. At one point no one was at the trunk of the car. A man ran from the west end of the street toward the car. He was traveling east. He grabbed a bag from the trunk of the car. This caused our dog, Jeremiah, to bark. The man dropped the bag and ran back toward the west end of the street. Jeremiah chased the man and stopped him. I saw the entire event as I ran after Jeremiah.

After police investigators took statements from Susy and Jim, photographers made photos of the crime scene. Your job is to observe these footprints and draw some inferences from them about who is telling the truth. Your inferences are very important because Jim wants to bring a lawsuit against Bobby for the damage he received from Bobby's dog.

Procedure

1. Use crayons to color the prints on the "Crime Scene Photograph." Color the prints as follows:

   #1—red
   #2—yellow
   #3—blue
   #4—orange
   #5—green

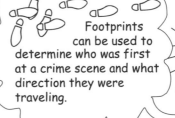

Footprints can be used to determine who was first at a crime scene and what direction they were traveling.

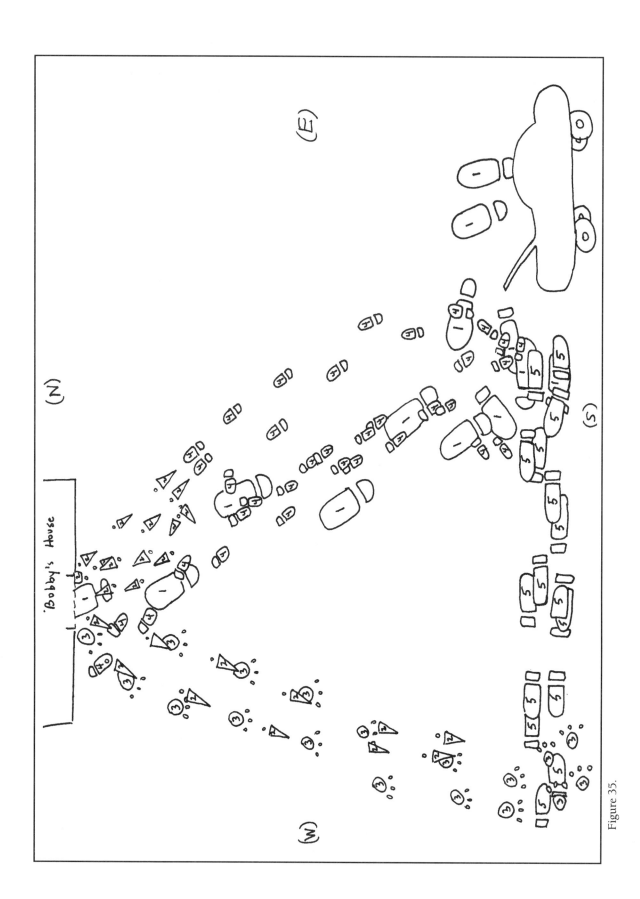

Figure 35.

2. Examine the footprint photograph (Figure 35), make observations, and record these observations in the Data Table.

DATA TABLE. OBSERVATIONS MADE FROM CRIME SCENE PHOTOGRAPH.	
Direction the house is from the car (select southwest, northwest, northeast, or southeast)	
Direction the car was traveling when it parked in front of the house (west or east)	
Which color footprints were the first ones made outside the trunk of the car?	
Which color footprints never made it all the way to the trunk of the car?	
Did the blue or yellow prints reach the green prints first?	
Which color print was made by the person driving the car?	
What direction or directions are the green prints traveling (west or east or both?)	

Conclusion Questions

1. Match the color of the print to the owner:

   ___ Yellow   a. Jeremiah

   ___ Orange   b. Bobby

   ___ Green   c. Susy

   ___ Blue   d. Jim

   ___ Red   e. Jesse

2. Which of the five individuals took groceries all the way from the car to the house?

   _____

   _____

3. Predict what Jesse did with the groceries he carried from the car.

   _____

   _____

   _____

   _____

4. Did Jim only walk towards the west by Bobby's house? If no, explain your answer.

   _____

   _____

   _____

   _____

5. Was Susy present to observe the dog's attack on Jim? How do you know?

   _____

   _____

   _____

   _____

6. Whose story is true: Jim's or Susy's? List all of the evidence that supports this person's story.

   _____

   _____

   _____

7. Write a one- or two-paragraph story explaining exactly what you think happened in the crime scene footprint drawing. Be sure to include all 5 characters and tell what they were doing.

_____

_____

_____

_____

_____

_____

_____

_____

_____

_____

_____

_____

_____

INVESTIGATION 4–4

FIBERS DON'T FIB

TEACHER INFORMATION

Audrey's dog Sam has a bad habit of grabbing neighbors' clothes off their clotheslines. Her neighbor Alanna is missing a new black dress, but Audrey can't find it anywhere. Students investigate by examining several types of black fibers found on Sam's rug and comparing them to a remnant from the lost dress.

Investigation Objectives:

Observe and study the physical properties of different fibers.
Compare crime scene fibers with known fibers.

Time Required: 50 minutes

Notes for the Teacher:

1. Read the Background to your students, then have them read The Crime.

2. Copy the Student Investigator Page for each student or for each group of students. You may want to sketch the appearance of some fibers on the chalkboard from Figure 36 or photocopy Figure 36 for your students to see the differences in fiber appearance. This activity is best done in groups of 2 or 3 students.

3. In preparation for the investigation, collect some single strands of fiber from the fabric store or from your home. Collect at least four different types of black fibers. Some suggestions include wool, silk, cotton, rayon, nylon, polyester, or Lycra™. Collect enough strands so each group has at least one of each of the four types. You should get twice as many strands of the fiber you select as the crime scene fiber. Each fiber sample should be the same length. Select fiber samples that are more than six inches long.

4. Label four plastic bags as A, B, C, and D. Label a fifth bag as CS for the crime scene. Once you have collected your fibers, place one of each type in plastic bags A through D. Place the fiber you collected twice as much of in Bag C. These four bags contain four different kinds of fibers found on Sam's rug at Audrey's house. In bag CS place the same type of fibers you put in Bag C. This will represent the sample of Alanna's dress.

> Fibers do not all look alike. Color, texture, shape, size, and strength are some ways to detect fiber type.

Background:

Fibers make up clothes, rugs, and some furniture. Many crimes that involve physical contact involve the transfer of fiber from one location to another. Fibers are often transferred between the clothing of a suspect and a victim. During hit-and-run car accidents, fibers from the clothes of the victim can be trapped on the bumper of the car. During robberies, fibers from clothing can become lodged on broken glass during a forced entry.

In the 1920s, rayon became the first manufactured fiber. Ten years later, over a dozen new fibers were developed for clothing and carpet. There are two main types of fiber: man-made and natural. Natural fibers are derived from plants and animals. The hair of sheep and rabbits are animal fibers while cotton is a plant fiber. Rayon and nylon are man-made fibers.

Fibers do not all look alike. They can be identified due to several properties. Color, texture, shape, size, and strength are a few ways you can detect a specific fiber type. Comparison of a fiber found at a crime scene with a fiber found on a suspect can help link that suspect with the scene of the crime.

Materials:

Bags of fibers A, B, C, and D (all taken from Sam's rug)
Bag of fibers from the dress (CS fibers)
Microscope
Hanging weights
5 pieces of white paper
Stereo microscope

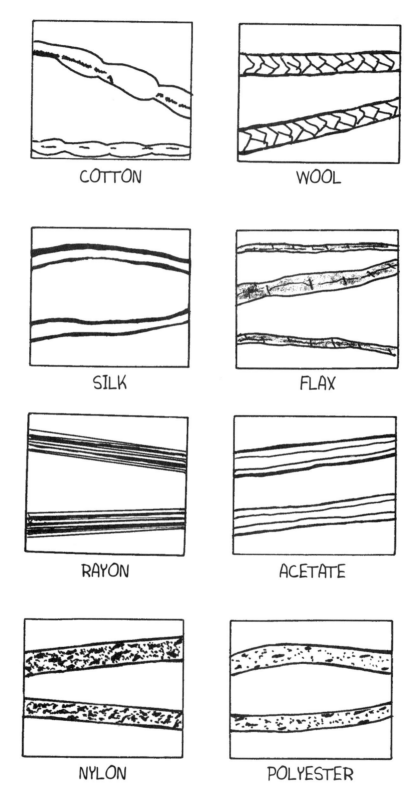

Figure 36. Some fibers and their appearance.

Answers to Conclusion Questions of Investigation 4–4:

1. yes; fiber C

2. Students can list any three of these five properties: color, texture, shape, size, and strength.

3. yes, because fibers matching the dress were found on Sam's rug

4. Answers will vary.

NSTA Objectives that apply to this investigation

As a result of activities in grades K–4, all students should develop:

- abilities necessary to do scientific inquiry and understanding about scientific inquiry. Students should employ simple equipment and tools to gather data and extend the senses. Students should use data to construct a reasonable explanation. (*Elementary Standard, Science as Inquiry*)

- abilities of technological design, understanding about science and technology, and abilities to distinguish between natural objects and objects made by humans. Students should understand fundamental concepts and principles that underlie the understanding about science and technology. Tools help scientists make better observations, measurements, and equipment for investigations. They help scientists see, measure, and do things that they could not otherwise see, measure, and do. (*Elementary Standard, Science and Technology*)

As a result of activities in grades 5–8, all students should develop:

- abilities necessary to do scientific inquiry and understandings about scientific inquiry. Students should use appropriate tools and techniques to gather, analyze, and interpret data. Students should think critically and logically to make the relationships between evidence and explanations. (*Grades 5–8 Standard, Science as Inquiry*)

- abilities necessary to do scientific inquiry and understandings about scientific inquiry. Students should understand fundamental concepts and principles that underlie the understanding about the abilities necessary to do scientific inquiry. Students should think critically and logically to make the relationships between evidence and explanations. Students should be able to review data from a simple experiment, summarize the data, and form a logical argument about the cause-and-effect relationships in the experiment. (*Grades 5–8 Standard, Science as Inquiry*)

- abilities necessary to do scientific inquiry and understandings about properties and changes of properties in matter, motions and forces, and transfer of energy. Students should understand fundamental concepts and principles that underlie the properties and changes of properties in matter. A substance has characteristic properties, such as density, boiling point, and solubility, all of which are independent of the amount of the sample. A mixture of substances often can be separated into the original substances using one or more of the characteristic properties. (*Grades 5–8 Standard, Physical Science*)

Name _____ Date _____

FIBERS DON'T FIB
STUDENT INVESTIGATOR PAGE

The Crime

Audrey's dog, Sam, is developing a bad reputation around the neighborhood. Sam loves to collect newspapers and bring them to Audrey. He has also brought Audrey some shirts and underwear from nearby clotheslines.

Sam has a specific routine for bringing his treasures home. First he carries his new prize to the rug outside the front door. He plays with it a little, then barks and bangs on the door for Audrey to come outside.

Alanna lives down the street from Audrey. Alanna hangs her clothes on the back porch to air dry. This morning Alanna hung a very expensive black dress in the breeze for a couple of hours. Alanna planned to wear the dress to an important banquet that evening. At noon when Alanna checked on the dress, it was gone. She immediately called the police.

When the police officer asked Alanna if she had noticed anything unusual around her house that morning, a thought came to her. She told the officer she saw her neighbor's beagle, Sam, lounging on the sidewalk in front of her house. Alanna said that Sam was known for stealing papers and clothing throughout the neighborhood. She gave the police a remnant of the lost dress, a piece she had kept when she hemmed the dress.

Police investigators walked to Audrey's house after talking to Alanna. They were greeted by a cute and energetic beagle named Sam. Audrey came to the door and listened intently while Alanna's story was explained by the police. Audrey and the police searched her garage and yard for the black dress, but didn't find it.

One of the officers suggested that they collect fibers from Sam's rug. Fibers were collected, placed in white paper, and labeled. Several types of black fibers were found on the rug. Police told Audrey they would compare the black fibers on Sam's rug to the black fibers from Alanna's dress. If a match is found, Audrey may need to pay Alanna for the missing dress.

> Fibers do not all look alike. Color, texture, shape, size, and strength are some ways to detect fiber type.

Procedure

1. Label five pieces of white paper as A, B, C, D, and CS.

2. Remove fiber A from bag A and place it on the paper. Remove fiber B from bag B and place it on the paper. Repeat this for fibers C, D, and CS.

3. Perform the following tests and record your observations in the Data Table.

    a. Record the color of the fibers in the Data Table. You may have different shades of black—from pale black to dark black.

    b. Place each fiber on the stereo microscope and sketch what you see in the Data Table under "appearance under microscope."

    c. Note the width or diameter of each fiber. Record the width of the fiber as "narrow" or "wide." You may have to compare several fibers to make this determination.

    d. Have your group partners hold one end of one of the fibers. Hold the fiber close to the floor or your desk. Place a small hanging weight on the fiber. Add more weights until the fiber breaks. Record how much weight was needed to break the fiber (Figure 37). Repeat this procedure for all five fibers.

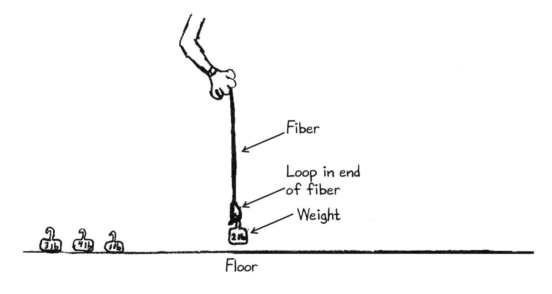

Figure 37. Testing the strength of fibers.

DATA TABLE. CHARACTERISTICS OF FIBERS.				
	Color	*Appearance under microscope*	*Diameter*	*Strength*
Fiber A				
Fiber B				
Fiber C				
Fiber D				
Crime Scene Fiber				

Conclusion Questions

1. Were there any fibers on Sam's rug that matched the missing dress? If so, which one matched?

   _____

   _____

2. Describe at least three properties investigators can use to compare fibers.

   _____

   _____

   _____

3. Is there evidence that Sam may have stolen the dress?

   _____

   _____

   _____

4. Complete this story in a one-paragraph conclusion describing the findings of the crime lab. Give evidence that Sam did or did not steal the dress. Recommend what Audrey should do about Alanna's dress, if anything.

   _____

   _____

   _____

   _____

   _____

   _____

INVESTIGATION 4–5

You're in Deep Trouble

Teacher Information

The principal suspects that someone has urinated in her flower pots and killed her flowers. Students test synthesized urine made from ammonia, vinegar, and food coloring to identify the culprit.

Investigation Objectives:

Conduct various tests on known urine samples to identify characteristics of urine. Identify the owner of an unknown urine sample.

Time Required: 50 minutes

Notes for the Teacher:

1. Read the Background to your students, then have them read The Crime.

2. Copy a Student Investigator Page for each student or for each group of students. This activity is best done in groups of 2 or 3 students.

3. Prepare five 1-liter containers of artificial urine. Mark each container with one of the following labels: Tom, Bill, Jerry, Dave, Flower Pot.

4. Pour 1 liter of distilled water into each container. Add the following additional items to each container:

   ■ Tom's urine—Add enough vinegar to make the pH lower than 5, and enough yellow food coloring to make the sample yellow.

   ■ Bill's urine—Add enough yellow food coloring to make the sample yellow and add enough ammonia to raise the pH to 7.1 or slightly higher.

   ■ Jerry's urine—Add enough green food coloring to make the sample a very pale green and a few spoonfuls of apple juice to provide a positive glucose test. Adjust the pH to about 6 by adding vinegar. Stir in some yeast cells to make the urine cloudy. After adding the yeast, check the pH and be sure it hasn't changed.

- Dave's urine—Add enough green to get the same color as seen in Jerry's urine. Make the pH 8 by adding ammonia as needed. Add yeast to this sample as you did to Jerry's to make it equally as cloudy.

- Flower pot urine—This sample should be exactly the same as Jerry's urine sample.

5. There are two ways to test for glucose:

- The easier, but more expensive, way is to use glucose test strips. These can be obtained through science supply houses or at a pharmacy.

- The more complicated, but less expensive, way is to add 10 drops of Benedict's solution to the urine sample in a test tube. Heat the test tube in a hot water bath for about 3 minutes. Results: no sugar—blue; trace of sugar—green; 1 to 2% of the urine contains sugar—yellow; more than 2% of the solution contains sugar—orange or red.

Background:

Urine can provide important information in a criminal investigation. Urine found at a crime scene might be useful as evidence. The chemicals in urine can vary from one individual to the next. Therefore, a person's urine can be unique enough to positively identify a suspect.

> Chemicals in urine can vary from one person to the next.

You can perform tests to determine some of the characteristics of a urine sample. We will examine three basic tests:

a. Visual observation of color and transparency are the first things to consider when comparing urine samples. Urine can have a variety of colors, ranging from colorless to amber. Urine color is related to the substances in the urine. Some diseases can cause different colors, too. Red or brown urine may indicate the presence of blood. Diabetics may have pale green urine.

The transparency of urine varies from one person to the next. Most urine is clear, but cloudy urine can result from normal bacteria or from abnormal pus in the urine.

b. The pH of urine is an important test. Urine pH usually ranges from 4.7 to 8.0. Most urine is acidic (has a pH less than 7). The pH of urine varies with the time of day, types of food consumed, and amount of water consumed. It can also be influenced by stress, tiredness, and rate of respiration. In the morning, urine is usually very acidic because of the buildup of carbon dioxide in the system. A lot of protein in the diet also causes urine to be acidic. Eating vegetables may cause urine to be alkaline (pH above 7).

c. A third urine test measures the presence of glucose. Glucose (blood sugar) can appear in the urine of people with diabetes. Diabetics have problems with insulin, a chemical in the body that helps it use glucose. You get energy from the breakdown of glucose in your cells. In diabetics, glucose cannot be taken from the blood into the cells where it is needed. Instead, it travels in the blood until it reaches the kidneys, where it is removed and expelled in urine. Diabetics who are not under treatment constantly have glucose in their urine. A diet high in sugar can temporarily cause glucose to appear in anyone's urine.

Materials:

Urine samples from Tom, Dave, Jerry, Bill, and the flower pot
5 strips of pH paper and color chart
5 glucose paper strips and color chart
White paper
5 test tubes
Test tube rack
Grease pencil or masking tape for labeling test tubes
Graduated cylinder
Medicine dropper

Answers to Conclusion Questions of Investigation 4–5:

1. Jerry; his urine produced the same test results as the flower pot urine

2. Tom and Jerry

3. Jerry; no; glucose can appear in urine after eating a lot of sugar

4. Answers will vary.

NSTA Objectives that apply to this investigation

As a result of the activities in grades K–4, all students should develop:

■ an understanding of properties of objects and materials, position and motion of objects, light, heat, electricity, and magnetism. Students should understand fundamental concepts and principles that underlie the properties of objects and materials. Objects have observable properties, including size, weight, shape, color, temperature, and the ability to react with other substances. (*Elementary Standard, Physical Science*)

■ abilities of technological design, understanding about science and technology, and abilities to distinguish between natural objects and objects made by humans. Students should understand fundamental concepts and principles that underlie the understanding about science and technology. Tools help scientists make better observations, measurements, and equipment for investigations. They help scientists see, measure, and do things that they could not otherwise see, measure, and do. (*Elementary Standard, Science and Technology*)

As a result of activities in grades 5–8, all students should develop:

- abilities necessary to do scientific inquiry and understanding about scientific inquiry. Students should understand fundamental concepts and principles that underlie the understanding about the abilities necessary to do scientific inquiry. Students should identify questions that can be answered through scientific investigations. Students should develop the ability to identify their questions with scientific ideas, concepts, and quantitative relationships that guide investigation. (*Grades 5–8 Standard, Science as Inquiry*)

- understanding of structure and function in living things, reproduction and heredity, regulation and behavior, populations and ecosystems, and diversity and adaptations of organisms. Students should understand fundamental concepts and principles that underlie the understanding of structure and function in living systems. The human organism has systems for digestion, respiration, reproduction, circulation, excretion, movement, control, and coordination, and for protection from disease. These systems interact with one another. (*Grades 5–8, Life Science*)

- abilities necessary to do scientific inquiry and understandings about scientific inquiry. Students should understand fundamental concepts and principles that underlie the understanding about the abilities necessary to do scientific inquiry. Students should think critically and logically to make the relationship between evidence and explanations. Students should be able to review data from a simple experiment, summarize the data, and form a logical argument about the cause-and-effect relationships in the experiment. (*Grades 5–8, Science as Inquiry*)

Name _____ Date _____

YOU'RE IN DEEP TROUBLE
STUDENT INVESTIGATOR PAGE

The Crime

Mrs. Fornwalt loves flowers. She places them in her office and waiting area. As the principal of a middle school, she wants her students to enjoy nature. Even students who are waiting to see her because they've misbehaved are surrounded by Mrs. Fornwalt's beautiful flowers. Unfortunately, for the last two weeks the flowers have been dying. Mrs. Fornwalt cannot decide what could be happening, but she suspects that students may be damaging her plants.

Mrs. Fornwalt asks her secretary for a list of all students who have been in her waiting area during the last two weeks. The secretary proudly produces names of seven students, many of whom were there several times last week.

This morning, Principal Fornwalt makes an interesting discovery. Four students are waiting in her office to see her because of behavior problems. As she opens the door to call Tom into her office, she notices an unusual smell. Looking around the room, she finds a yellow liquid in the bottom of a flower pot. This surprises her since she didn't water the plants today. Suddenly she recognizes the smell and realizes that someone urinated in her flower pot.

Mrs. Fornwalt questions the four boys in the waiting area, but no one will admit the foul deed. She checks the list of names of previous visitors and finds that all four boys have been to see her several times in the past two weeks. She feels sure that one of them is her flower killer.

Mrs. Fornwalt has an idea that might solve this mystery. She calls the school nurse in to help her. The nurse agrees, and asks all four boys to give her a urine sample in a paper cup. She also collects urine from the flower pot, and pours it into another paper cup.

You can help Mrs. Fornwalt determine who urinated in her flowers.

Procedure

1. Label the five test tubes as:

   T for Tom's urine

   B for Bill's urine

   J for Jerry's urine

   D for Dave's urine

   FP for urine in the flower pot

Chemicals in urine can vary from one person to the next.

2. Place 10 milliliters of each urine sample in the appropriate test tube. Stand the five tubes in the test tube rack.

3. Hold a piece of white paper behind the five test tubes. In the Data Table, record the color of each sample. (Colors could include colorless, bright yellow, dark yellow, amber, yellow-orange, pale green, black, brown, and red.) Also note and record the transparency (clarity) of each sample. (Transparencies include clear, slightly cloudy, very cloudy, and opaque.)

4. Tear off a strip of pH paper and dip it into test tube T. Once it has air dried for 10 seconds, compare the color of the paper with the color chart. On the Data Table, indicate the pH of the urine. Repeat this step for the other four samples.

5. Test the urine samples for the presence of sugar by dipping a glucose test strip in each. Consult the bottle that accompanies the test strips to interpret your results. Record these in the Data Table. If no glucose is present, write "negative" in the Data Table. (If glucose test strips are not available, consult your teacher for another procedure to test for glucose.)

DATA TABLE. COLOR, TRANSPARENCY, PH, AND GLUCOSE RESULTS ON FIVE URINE SAMPLES.			
Sample	*Color and transparency*	*pH*	*Presence of Glucose*
Tom			
Bill			
Jerry			
Dave			
Flower Pot			

Conclusion Questions

1. Who was the criminal? Explain your answer.

   _____

   _____

   _____

2. Name the suspects who had acidic urine.

   _____

   _____

   _____

3. List the suspects who had glucose in their urine. Does this mean they were diabetics? Explain your answer.

   _____

   _____

   _____

4. In one or two paragraphs, write a conclusion to this story. Name your criminal and the evidence you have against him. Describe how you will present this case to the parents of the criminal.

   _____

   _____

   _____

   _____

   _____

   _____

   _____

INVESTIGATION 4–6
GUILTY OF GRAFFITI

TEACHER INFORMATION

A student has scrawled graffiti across a workbook in Mrs. Platt's language arts class. Students help Mrs. Platt find the graffiti artist by making chromatograms from suspect students' ink pens and comparing them to the ink on the workbook.

Investigation Objectives:

Separate the colors of water-soluble inks.
Compare crime scene ink with suspects' ink.

Time Required: 50 minutes

Notes for the Teacher:

1. Read the Background to your students, then have them read The Crime.

2. Copy the Student Investigator Page for each group of students. This activity is best done in groups of 2 or 3 students.

3. Choose six different brands of water-soluble black ink pens to produce six different chromatograms. Label each pen with a separate name: Steven, Spencer, Matt, Audrey, Sharon, and Peggy. Select the pen you labeled as "Steven" to write the note that represents the sample from the vandalized workbook.

4. You may want to use colored chalk and sketch Figure 38 from the Background on the chalkboard prior to doing this activity.

Background:

Ink that dissolves in water is called "water soluble." Water-soluble black ink is a mixture of several different colors of ink. If you write your name on a napkin with a water-soluble black ink pen and then let a few drops of water fall on your name, you will find that the black ink separates into colors. The pattern of colors formed by the ink is called a chromatogram. Different brands of ink produce different chromatograms.

Chromatograms can help detect forgery. If you copy or reproduce someone else's handwriting without his or her permission, you may be guilty of forgery. If the same pen was used to write an entire document, ink samples taken from two different places on a document should produce identical chromatograms. However, if different pens were used, the chromatograms would be different. This chromatogram evidence suggests that part of the document may have been forged.

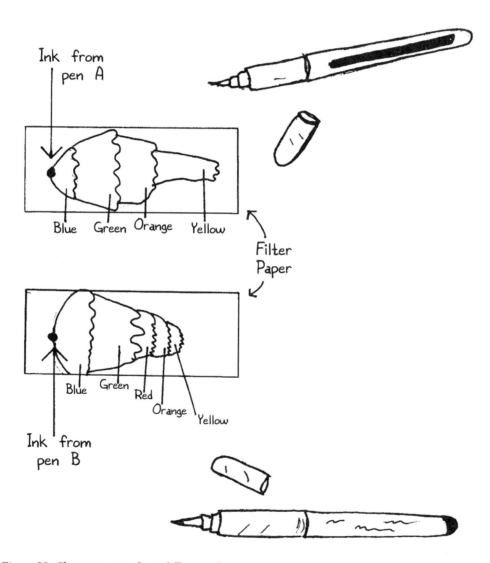

Figure 38. Chromatograms from different ink pens.

Materials:

6 water-soluble black ink pens labeled with names
Scissors
6 strips of filter paper
Jar or beaker
Strip of paper from the vandalized workbook (prepared from one of the six black ink pens)
Water
Ruler

Answers to Conclusion Questions of Investigation 4–6:

1. one; Steven

2. A chromatogram is a pattern of colors produced when ink is dissolved in water.

3. "Water soluble" means able to dissolve in water.

4. The chromatogram of one location on a document can be compared with the chromatogram from the questioned portion of the document to see if a different pen had been used.

5. to dissolve the black ink mixture and separate it into its colors

6. Answers will vary.

NSTA Objectives that apply to this investigation

As a result of activities in grades K–4, all students should develop:

- abilities necessary to do scientific inquiry and understanding about scientific inquiry. Students should employ simple equipment and tools to gather data and extend the senses. Students should use data to construct a reasonable explanation. (*Elementary Standard, Science as Inquiry*)

- abilities necessary to do scientific inquiry and understanding about scientific inquiry. Students should use data to construct a reasonable explanation. (*Elementary Standard, Science as Inquiry*)

- understanding of personal health, characteristics and changes in population, types of resources, changes in environments, and science and technology in local challenges. Students should understand fundamental concepts and principles that underlie the understanding about changes in environments. Changes in environments can be natural or influenced by humans. Pollution is a change in the environment that can influence the health, survival, or activities of organisms, including humans. (*Elementary Standard, Science in Personal and Social Perspectives*)

As a result of activities in grades 5–8, all students should develop:

- abilities necessary to do scientific inquiry and understandings about scientific inquiry. Students should use appropriate tools and techniques to gather, analyze, and interpret data. Students should think critically and logically to make the relationships between evidence and explanations. (*Grades 5–8 Standard, Science as Inquiry*)

- abilities necessary to do scientific inquiry and understandings about scientific inquiry. Students should understand fundamental concepts and principles that underlie the understanding about the abilities necessary to do scientific inquiry. Students should identify questions that can be answered through scientific investigations. Students should develop the ability to identify their questions with scientific ideas, concepts, and quantitative relationships that guide investigation. (*Grades 5–8 Standard, Science as Inquiry*)

- abilities necessary to do scientific inquiry and understandings about scientific inquiry. Students should understand fundamental concepts and principles that underlie the understanding about the abilities necessary to do scientific inquiry. Students should think critically and logically to make the relationships between evidence and explanations. Students should be able to review data from a simple experiment, summarize the data, and form a logical argument about the cause-and-effect relationships in the experiment. (*Grades 5–8 Standard, Science as Inquiry*)

- abilities necessary to do scientific inquiry and understandings about scientific inquiry. Students should understand fundamental concepts and principles that underlie the understanding about the abilities necessary to do scientific inquiry. Students should use appropriate tools and techniques to gather, analyze, and interpret data. (*Grades 5–8, Science as Inquiry*)

- understanding of science as a human endeavor, nature of science, and history of science. Students should understand fundamental concepts and principles that underlie the understanding of the nature of science. It is part of scientific inquiry to evaluate the results of scientific investigations, experiments, observations, theoretical models, and the explanations proposed by other scientists. (*Grades 5–8 Standard, History and Nature of Science*)

- abilities necessary to do scientific inquiry and understandings about properties and changes of properties in matter, motions and forces, and transfer of energy. Students should understand fundamental concepts and principles that underlie the properties and changes of properties in matter. A substance has characteristic properties, such as density, boiling point, and solubility, all of which are independent of the amount of the sample. A mixture of substances often can be separated into the original substances using one or more of the characteristic properties. (*Grades 5–8 Standard, Physical Science*)

Name _____ Date _____

GUILTY OF GRAFFITI
STUDENT INVESTIGATOR PAGE

The Crime

In Mrs. Platt's English class, students work at tables in groups of six. Today Mrs. Platt hands out brand new workbooks to students at Table B. She also gives each student at Table B a black ink pen with his or her name on it. Sharon, Steven, Peggy, Matt, Spencer, and Audrey sit at Table B.

In the hour before lunch, students at Table B work individually in their workbooks. When the lunch bell rings, students stack their workbooks and pens in the middle of the table. Mrs. Platt and her class reach the lunch line before she realizes that her pocketbook is back in the classroom.

Mrs. Platt returns to the room to get her purse from the closet. As she crosses the room. something at Table B catches her eye. She walks over to the stack of workbooks and picks up the one on top. To her horror, "Mrs. Platt is a Rat!" has been written across the front of the workbook in black ink.

During lunch Mrs. Platt develops a plan to discover the workbook vandal. Back in the classroom, she asks that the guilty member of Table B step forward. Nothing happens. Mrs. Platt decides to change this English class disaster into a science lesson. She collects the pens and the vandalized workbook from Table B. She uses scissors to cut a small section from the vandalized part of the workbook. She moistens this section in water and places it on a piece of white paper to dry.

Mrs. Platt cuts a piece of paper into six strips. With a pencil, she labels each strip with the name of each student at Table B. Then she uses each student's pen to mark on the appropriate strip. Each strip is then dipped in water. The chromatograms that result from this test point to the guilty party.

Procedure

1. Pour enough water into the jar to cover the bottom.

2. Place the workbook strip in the jar so the ink end barely contacts the water. The opposite end will hang over the side of the jar (Figure 39). Water should not touch the ink on the workbook strip of paper.

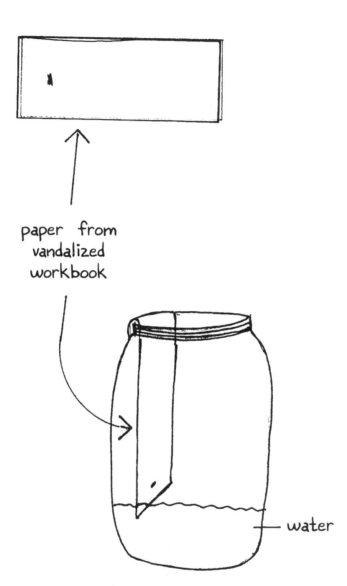

Figure 39. The strip of paper from the vandalized workbook in the jar of water.

Don't allow the ink dots to drop into the water when lowering the paper to the water.

3. Watch the jar for ten minutes or until water is absorbed up most of the length of the strip.

4. Remove the strip of paper and place it on white paper to dry.

5. Gather six strips of filter paper and a pencil. Place one of the following names on one end of each of the six strips: Sharon, Matt, Spencer, Audrey, Peggy, and Steven.

6. Using each student's pen, place a large dot of ink on the appropriate strip. Place the dot about 2 cm from the opposite end of the strip where you wrote the name (Figure 40).

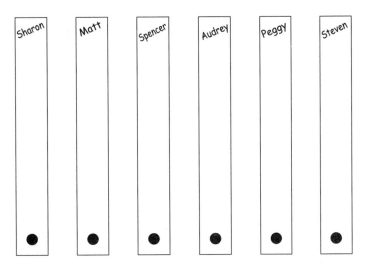

Figure 40. The six filter paper strips, complete with names and ink dots.

7. Place each strip around the inside of the jar so that each ink end barely contacts the water. The opposite end will hang over the side of the jar (Figure 41). Water should not touch the ink.

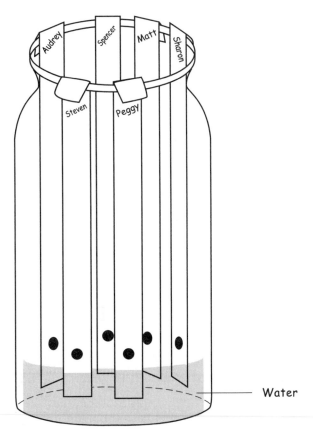

Figure 41. The strips from each ink pen are placed in the jar so the ink barely contacts the water. The opposite end hangs over the lip of the jar.

8. Watch the jar for ten minutes or until water is absorbed up the length of most of the strips.

9. Remove the strips of paper and place them on white paper to dry.

10. Compare the chromatograms produced by each ink pen with the chromatogram from the vandalized workbook.

Conclusion Questions

1. How many of the six chromatograms match the chromatogram from the vandalized workbook? List the matching names.

_____

_____

_____

2. In your own words, describe what is meant by the term "chromatogram."

_____

_____

_____

3. Explain what the term "water-soluble" means.

_____

_____

4. How can chromatograms help detect forgery?

_____

_____

5. What was the purpose of dipping the ink strips in water?

_____

_____

6. Write a one-paragraph conclusion to The Crime.

_____

_____

_____

_____

_____

_____

INVESTIGATION 4–7

THE BAFFLED BAKER

TEACHER INFORMATION

Barry's Bakery has had recent customer complaints that the pastries are less than tasty. Students run tests on unknown powders—baking soda, salt, corn starch, and powdered sugar—to help Barry find out what's wrong and keep his customers.

Investigation Objectives:

Observe some chemical and physical properties of substances.
Identify unknown powders through comparison of their properties with properties of known substances.

Time Required: 50 minutes

Notes for the Teacher:

1. Read the Background to your students, then have them read The Crime.

2. Copy a Student Investigator Page and figures 42 and 43 for each student or for each group of students. This activity is best done in groups of 2 or 3 students.

3. Prior to the investigation, discuss the difference in physical and chemical properties and review some examples.

4. In preparation for the investigation, prepare eight containers. Four of the containers will hold your "knowns." Place salt in one container, powdered sugar in one, baking soda in one, and corn starch in one. Mark the containers with the name of the substance each contains.

5. Prepare your four "unknowns" in the other four large containers. Label them as A, B, C, and D. In container "A" place some baking soda, in container "B" place salt, in container "C" place corn starch, and in "D" place powdered sugar. Each container should have its own separate spoon for dipping.

239

6. Use Lugol's solution as your iodine solution. If you do not have Lugol's solution, you can use medicinal iodine from the grocery store.

Background:

One job of scientists in crime labs is to identify unknown substances. Identification of an unknown can be made by testing the unknown's physical and chemical properties.

Physical properties of a substance can be observed without changing the identity of that substance. Weight, color, melting point, boiling point, density, and volume are some physical properties.

Comparing physical and chemical properities of "known" substances with "unknown" substances can help identify a chemical.

Chemical properties describe a substance when it reacts with other substances. Baking powder reacts with the ingredients in cake batter to produce carbon dioxide gas. This gas makes the cake rise. The ability of the baking powder to produce carbon dioxide gas in cake batter is a chemical property of baking powder.

An Alka Seltzer® tablet has both physical and chemical properties. Some physical properties of a tablet include its round shape and its density of more than 1 g/ml. The ability of the tablets to combine with water to produce carbon dioxide gas is a chemical property.

The physical and chemical properties of an unknown substance can help scientists identify that substance. Scientists already know the physical and chemical properties of many chemicals. As a result, they can compare properties of known substances with the properties of substances they are seeking to identify.

Materials:

Hand lens
Salt
Powdered sugar
Corn starch
Baking soda
Vinegar
Water
Iodine solution
2 16-well plates for each group
Toothpicks
Black paper

Answers to Conclusion Questions of Investigation 4–7

1. A—baking soda; B—salt; C—corn starch; D—powdered sugar

2. Color and shape are physical properties. They are helpful in identifying unknowns. Answers may vary, but they may say that color and shape helped them identify all of the powders.

3. Answers may vary. For example, they could describe the test that adds vinegar to the powders. Vinegar reacts with some of the powders to cause a chemical change, and gas is produced.

4. Answers will vary.

NSTA Objectives that apply to this investigation

As a result of the activities in grades K–4, all students should develop:

- an understanding of properties of objects and materials, position and motion of objects, light, heat, electricity, and magnetism. Students should understand fundamental concepts and principles that underlie the properties of objects and materials. Objects have observable properties, including size, weight, shape, color, temperature, and the ability to react with other substances. (*Elementary Standard, Physical Science*)

As a result of activities in grades 5–8, all students should develop:

- abilities necessary to do scientific inquiry and understandings about scientific inquiry. Students should understand fundamental concepts and principles that underlie the understanding about the abilities necessary to do scientific inquiry. Students should identify questions that can be answered through scientific investigations. Students should develop the ability to identify their questions with scientific ideas, concepts, and quantitative relationships that guide investigation. (*Grades 5–8 Standard, Science as Inquiry*)

- abilities necessary to do scientific inquiry and understandings about scientific inquiry. Students should understand fundamental concepts and principles that underlie the understanding about the abilities necessary to do scientific inquiry. Students should think critically and logically to make the relationship between evidence and explanations. Students should be able to review data from a simple experiment, summarize the data, and form a logical argument about the cause-and-effect relationships in the experiment. (*Grades 5–8, Science as Inquiry*)

- abilities necessary to do scientific inquiry and understandings about properties and changes of properties in matter, motions and forces, and transfer of energy. Students should understand fundamental concepts and principles that underlie the properties and changes of properties in matter. Substances react chemically in characteristic ways with other substances to form new substances with different characteristic properties. (*Grades 5–8 Standard, Physical Science*)

Name _____ Date _____

THE BAFFLED BAKER

STUDENT INVESTIGATOR PAGE

The Crime

Barry's Bakery is losing many of its long-time customers. For the past four weeks, customers have complained to Barry that his pastries taste funny. Barry is baffled. He doesn't know why the quality of his pastries is declining.

Barry has employed the same cook since the bakery opened five years ago. The cook's recipe has not changed in that five-year period. The only change at the bakery is the new manager, Lee Lazarus.

Barry is concerned about Lee's ability to manage the bakery. Two months ago Barry told Lee that he had to become more dependable if he wanted to keep his job. Lee had fallen behind on his work. Lee is responsible for incoming materials. He unpacks food supplies and places them in large canisters for the cook.

News around the bakery was that Lee did not take Barry's advice seriously. So Barry thought it might be a good idea to check Lee's work. Barry called in a private investigator to pose as an assistant cook to watch for anything unusual.

After a week of undercover work, the investigator had nothing to report. But Barry's customers were still complaining. The investigator told Barry that the cook was not to blame because he was following the recipes exactly.

Late one night, the investigator decided to test the ingredients used in the pastries. He wondered if some of the ingredients might be in the wrong containers. The investigator bought some powdered sugar, baking soda, salt, and corn starch—the main ingredients used in the pastries. He called these the "known" powders and tested them to find their physical and chemical properties.

Then he took samples of the powders in the baker's four canisters. He labeled these samples A, B, C, and D and called them the "unknowns." Help the Investigator by testing the known and unknown powders. Then you can decide whether or not Lee is putting the wrong ingredients in the canisters.

Procedure

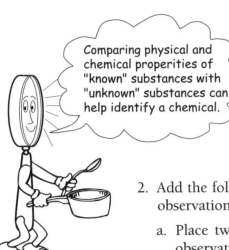

Comparing physical and chemical properities of "known" substances with "unknown" substances can help identify a chemical.

Part A. Physical and chemical properties of known powders

1. Place a 16-well plate beside Figure 42. Place the known white powders in their proper location in your well plate, following the diagram in Figure 42. Fill each well plate about half full with the appropriate powder.

2. Add the following to the appropriate wells. Observe and record your observation in Data Table 1.

   a. Place two drops of vinegar in wells 1, 2, 3, and 4. Record your observations in Data Table 1, under "Vinegar."

   b. Add two drops of iodine solution to wells 5, 6, 7, and 8. Record your observations under "Iodine" in Data Table 1.

   c. Add two drops of water to wells 9, 10, 11, and 12. Stir each well with a separate toothpick. Record your observations under "Water" in Data Table 1.

3. Remove a bit of powder from wells 13, 14, 15, and 16 and place each on a small piece of black paper. Keep the four samples separated while on the paper. Observe each for color. Use a hand lens to observe the individual crystals. Record your observations under "Color and shape" in Data Table 1.

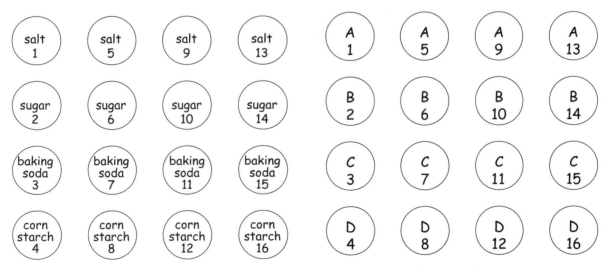

Figure 42. Known powders.   Figure 43. Unknown powders.

DATA TABLE 1. KNOWN POWDERS.				
	Vinegar	*Iodine*	*Water*	*Color and shape*
Salt	1	5	9	13
Sugar	2	6	10	14
Baking soda	3	7	11	15
Corn starch	4	8	12	16

Part B. Testing unknown powders

1. Place your second well plate beside the diagram in Figure 43.

2. Place the unknown white powders in their proper location according to the diagram. Fill each well half full with the powders.

3. Add the following to the appropriate wells. Observe and record your observations in Data Table 2.

   a. Place two drops of vinegar into wells 1, 2, 3, and 4. Record your observations under "Vinegar" in Data Table 2.

   b. Add two drops of iodine solution to wells 5, 6, 7, and 8. Record your observations under "Iodine" in Data Table 2.

   c. Add two drops of water to wells 9, 10, 11, and 12. Stir each well with a separate toothpick. Record your observations under "Water" in Data Table 2.

4. Remove a bit of powder from wells 13, 14, 15, and 16 and place each on a small piece of black paper. Keep the four samples separated while on the paper. Observe each for color. Use a hand lens to observe the individual crystals. Record your observations under "Color and shape" in Data Table 2.

	Vinegar	*Iodine*	*Water*	*Color and shape*
Unknown A	1	5	9	13
Unknown B	2	6	10	14
Unknown C	3	7	11	15
Unknown D	4	8	12	16

DATA TABLE 2. UNKNOWN POWDERS.

5. Compare Data Table 1 with Data Table 2 as you answer the Conclusion Questions.

6. Dispose of the materials in the two well plates in the location designated by your teacher.

Conclusion Questions

1. Identify the unknown powders:

   A _____

   B _____

   C _____

   D _____

2. In the last column on both data tables, you recorded the color and shape of crystals. Are *color* and *shape* physical or chemical properties?

   _____

   _____

   Did these properties help you identify any unknowns?

   _____

   _____

If so, which ones?

_____

_____

3. Describe one of the tests you performed on the unknown powders that revealed a chemical property. Explain your answer.

_____

_____

_____

_____

4. Complete this crime story in one or more paragraphs. Explain whether or not Barry should confront Lee with this evidence. In your paragraph(s) explain what you think happened to make the pastries taste bad at the bakery.

_____

_____

_____

_____

_____

_____

_____

Glossary

Acid   A substance with a pH less than 7 such as vinegar. The opposite of base. (*See* Investigation 2-2 for a clear definition and a scale with every-day examples.)

Alkaline   A base forming substance with pH greater than 7 which is capable of neutralizing acids.(*See* Base.)

Anatomy   The science of the structure of animals or plants. Dissection of an animal or plant to understand the position and structure of its parts.

Assailant   Attacker. A person who attacks either physically or with words as in arguments, doubts or questions.

Base   A substance with a pH greater than 7. The opposite of acid.

Biology   The science that deals with the study of plants and animals.

Calcium   One of the nutrients required by living things.

Carbon dioxide   A gas, each molecule of which contains one carbon atom and two oxygen atoms. Carbon dioxide is produced as a result of respiration in many living things.

Centimeter   A unit of the metric system used to measure length. One centimeter equals 1/100th of a meter. It is also equivalent to 2.54 inches.

Chromatogram   In paper chromatography, a strip of paper that shows the components of a mixture as separate stripes.

Chromosomes   Carry the genes that convey hereditary characteristics, and are constant in number for each species.

Confiscate   To seize private property by authority, usually as a penalty.

Cortex   The middle layer of the hair, between the cuticle and the inner medulla. Pigments in the cortex give the hair its color.

Cuticle   The outside layer of a strand of hair which consists of overlapping scales. Human and animal hair cuticles have different patterns of scales and are used to identify the type of the hair.

Debris   Rough, broken pieces of garbage, rubble, litter, or discarded remains of something. Artificial debris might be pieces of man-made items, like glass, found in a natural environment such as soil or water.

DNA   Deoxyribonucleic Acid. The basic material in the chromosomes of the cell nucleus. It contains the genetic code and transmits the hereditary pattern.

False advertisement   A claim or statement about a product that is not true.

Ecosystem   A system made up of a community of animals, plants, and bacteria interrelated together with its physical and chemical environment.

Fingerprint   An impression of the pattern on the inner surface of the fingertip used to identify people. The three basic patterns are loops, ridges, and whorls.

Forensics   The application of scientific methods and knowledge to legal matters, as in the investigation of a crime.

Forgery   Something (false) used for purposes of deception or fraud. To imitate or counterfeit documents, signatures, works of art, etc. with the intention to deceive.

Gene   Specific units on a chromosome that carry hereditary traits.

Glucose   A simple, six-carbon sugar.

Graffiti   Words or pictures written, scratched or drawn in an inappropriate location.

Hair follicle   An organ that is part of the skin, out of which the hair shaft extends from the root within the follicle. The hair shaft is made of three parts: cuticle, medulla, and cortex.

Heredity   The transmission of characteristics from parents to offspring by means of genes in the chromosomes.

Hydronium paper   Paper that indicates the pH of a solution. (*See* pH Scale.)

Hypothesis   An unproved theory offered to explain a set of facts.

Hypothetical   A supposition based on or relating to a hypothesis.

Imperfection   A characteristic such as a defect, fault or blemish that keeps something from being perfect. A flaw or superficial mark in a surface that detracts from an otherwise fine appearance.

Inference   A conclusion drawn from evidence or a conclusion reached by reasoning from something known or assumed.

Insulation   A material that prevents the escape of heat, electricity, sound, etc.

Legitimate   Authentic, real, genuine, reasonable or logically correct.

Lye   The common name of a very strong corrosive chemical agent, sodium hydroxide. Very dangerous to living things.

Magnesium   An element in the soil that is essential for plant growth. It is part of chlorophyll, the pigment necessary for plants to make their own food.

Medulla   A collection of cells that has the appearance of a central canal running through a hair. The pattern and diameter of the medulla can be used to distinguish between an animal and a human hair sample.

Milliliters   A metric unit for measuring volume of 1/1000th of a liter. 1,000 milliliters equals 1 liter.

Morse Code   A code made up of dots and dashes, short and long sounds or flashes of light that represent letters and numbers. Was designed to be used on the telegraph, one of our earliest forms of communication over wires.

Neutral   A substance, such as pure distilled water, with a pH of 7. neither acid, nor base.

Nitrogen   An element in the soil that is essential for plant growth. Plants deficient in nitrogen have stunted growth and yellow-green leaves.

Palmate   The vein pattern on a leaf that has all main veins extending from the base of the leaf.

Patent   A patent is a grant made by the government to an inventor, assuring the inventor of the sole right to use and sell the invention for a certain time period.

Petri dish   A round, clear dish with a top used in a laboratory.

Phosphorus   An element in the soil essential for plant growth. Phosphorus-deficient plants grow slowly and new growth is often spindly and brittle.

pH Scale   A scale from 1 to 14 used to measure degree of acidity or alkalinity. On this scale, 0 to .699 is acidic; 7 is neutral; 7.01 to 14 is alkaline (basic).

Pinnate   A vein pattern on a leaf that consists of one main vein with other smaller veins extending from it.

Plasticine   Material that can easily be molded into a specific shape.

Scientific Method of Problem Solving   A 6-step system of problem-solving. 1) State the hypothesis or problem; 2) Research the problem; 3) Design and conduct an experiment to test your hypothesis; 4) Gather data; 5) Draw conclusions; 6) Report your findings.

Sodium hydroxide   A strong base with a pH of 14 as in drain cleaner.

Transparency   The degree to which a material can transmit light rays so that objects on one side of that material may be distinctly seen from the other side.

Vandalism   Persons who deface or destroy others' property.

Venation   The pattern of veins in a leaf. Veins carry water and minerals to tissues throughout the leaf.

Vertebral   Refers to the small bones that make up the spinal column or backbone.

Vertical   Straight up and down. Opposite to horizontal or across.

Water-soluble   A material that can be dissolved in water.